T0244908

ANOTHER MOVE, GOD?

BETH RUNKLE

ANOTHER

MOVE,

GOD?

30 Encouragements to Embrace Your Life as a
★ MILITARY WIFE ★

B&H
PUBLISHING®
BRENTWOOD, TENNESSEE

This book is dedicated to the important people who made my journey as a military wife possible:

To my warrior, Bryan, who invited me to stand by his side through the adventures of military life and patiently waited for me to embrace his calling.

and

To my favorite people—military wives who support one another and serve as the home-front heroes while our military men battle on the front lines.

Acknowledgments

To Jesus: I am thankful that you met me and showed me your love and care when I first studied Genesis. Thank you for meeting me in the pages of your life-giving Word and more importantly, for dying in my place to take the penalty for my sin. You are so worthy, and I praise you. Anything "good" written in this book is due to the Holy Spirit at work in my life. You deserve all the glory!

To the Father: Thank you that I've always been able to cling to your sovereignty amid the chaos of military life. I never could have done it without you as my Rock! Thank you for creating me with a desire to learn so that I could eventually use my brain to study your Word and point others to you.

To my husband: Thank you for standing by my side and cheering me on during this journey. I'm so appreciative of your support and for all of the extra duties you took on to give me time for writing and theology courses.

To my kids: Brody, Grace, and Noelle, thanks for your support and encouragement. Thank you also for patiently helping me learn Instagram so I can reach more young spouses of the military.

To my prayer team: I know it was your prayers that enabled me to finish this journey. Please continue praying that this book will get into the hands of the young military wives who need to know the Lord and his control over their lives. I'm truly grateful for your prayers. Thank you: Far, Carleene, Karen, Carrie, Joan, Janell, Lynn, Kelly, Molly, Suzanne, Patty, Christine, Jamie, Todd, Marty, Corinne, Bryan, Kathy, Wendi, Angela, Ellie, Cathy, Jennifer, Laurie, Tara, Dallas, Isabel, Emily, Marla, Michelle, Linda, Kellie, Paula, Stephanie, Chris, Pam, and Erin.

To my dear friends, Kelly Moore and Tara Williams, whose husbands still both serve in the US Military: our friendship has been a great gift. Thank you for supporting me as I pursued this call from the Lord. Your encouragement, support, and prayers are so appreciated. I'm blessed to call you both friends.

To Amy Harris: Thanks for being my younger military wife friend who gave me such great advice and help along the way. You are an amazing person; I'm so glad to call you a friend!

To the ladies who have served as a mentor to me: First, to Lucinda Seacrest McDowell, who is no longer on this side of eternity; I'm so grateful for your investment in me. I firmly believe this book would have not been in print without your superb coaching and encouragement. I wish you were here in person for me to hug and thank. You were a true gem of a person, so selfless and encouraging. Thank you to Ellie Kay for your advice and expertise along the way. We only lived on the same military base for nine months yet have remained close friends. You have been with me and helped me with every step of this journey. Thank you also to Pam Farrell and Mary R. Snyder who helped coach me in this writing journey. Thank you both for being willing to invest me in. I know your time is precious, and it was a gift to me!

To Carol Kent and Bonnie Emmorey: Thank you for leading, organizing, and hosting the Speak Up Conference each year. This book would never have come about if I had not attended Speak Up several times. I know there are countless other authors with the same testimony. I continue to be blessed by both of you, your love for the Lord, and your investment in Christian speakers and writers.

To the women of the Protestant Women of the Chapel (PWOC) at each military installation where I've been involved: I love forming relationships with and studying God's Word with each of you. Thank you for being my sisters in Christ.

To the online Bible study group, I created during COVID who studied the Bible with me for four years: Your love for deeply engaging with the Word of God helped propel me to enroll in Seminary which led to this book. You all are so dear to me.

To Dan Balow, my agent: Thank you so much for being willing to take a chance with me and market a book specifically for military wives. Your efforts have been a gift to me and our military community.

To Ashley Gorman and the rest of the staff at B&H Publishing Group: It has been a joy and a blessing to work with you. Thank you for the opportunity to publish with you.

Contents

A Word from Beth xiii

Introduction 1

Day 1: Lingering Loneliness. 5

Day 2: Stick like Glue. 11

Day 3: Being an Influencer. 17

Day 4: Life-Giving Counterpart 21

Day 5: Tent-Dwellers 27

Day 6: Set-Apart Lives 31

Day 7: Where's Your Focus? 37

Day 8: Climb on the Altar 41

Day 9: Peace over Possessions. 47

Day 10: Your Spiritual Weapon 53

Day 11: Fortify Yourself 59

Day 12: Faith over Fear 65

Day 13: Waiting 71

Day 14: Declared Righteous............................77

Day 15: Covenant..................................83

Day 16: Flourishing vs. Fierce 89

Day 17: The God Who Sees...........................95

Day 18: Hard Roads................................99

Day 19: Building a Legacy 105

Day 20: Single Parenting 111

Day 21: Hospitality................................117

Day 22: Unbelief..................................123

Day 23: Humility and Vulnerability....................129

Day 24: Intercession 135

Day 25: Salty.....................................141

Day 26: God's Protection 147

Day 27: God of the Impossible.......................153

Day 28: Prompt Obedience 159

Day 29: The Lord Will Provide.......................165

Day 30: Ending Well 171

Notes...177

A Word from Beth

Have you often thought how different your life would be if you weren't moving so frequently and adjusting to fit into the military? Do you wish you could feel more settled? Yet in all the unpacking and packing, you've lost your heart somewhere along the way?

I am with you! I've often thought about what it would look like to have lived a "normal life" in which uncertainty and change were not the only constants in my life. My husband served on active duty for twenty-five years in the Air Force, during which we moved fourteen times. As a military wife, I see you trying to make the best of your moves and support your family, and I am with you in an uncertain and chaotic life.

While there are many books you could pick up to help you navigate military life from many different angles, I want to help you face military life's changes and unique opportunities from a spiritual perspective. This book will address ways to help you get a handle on this transient life with insights from women in the Bible who seem to have faced many of the same challenges military wives face.

I began my faith journey by studying the book of Genesis. God grabbed my attention as I saw the many parallels between the life of Sarah and my life. I was a new military spouse whose husband had just deployed three times in our first two and a half years of marriage. I identified with Sarah's life as I found frequent parallels between her seminomadic lifestyle and mine. As we glean from her story in the pages that follow, I hope this book will meet you where you are and address some of your feelings, insecurities, and weaknesses—especially those that come with being called by God to a military marriage.

As you read through this book, I encourage you to begin your day by reading the Scriptures referenced from the book of Genesis and selected New Testament verses. I pray that as you seek the Lord for whom he has called you to be as a military wife, and that you will see yourself in his kingdom army. God's assignment is for you and your husband to serve the Lord and his people where the military has assigned you. May this be a time of exponential growth for you!

Although you can work through this book on your own, a great way to engage more with the content is to grab a friend or group of friends who can work through the book with you. In that case, I'd recommend you seek to complete five days of the study each week and gather with a friend or friends each week for discussion. I have created a leader's guide to enhance your discussion and group meetings. You can access this free resource at https://www.BethRunkle.com.

I will be praying for you as you walk through this journey. I pray that God will speak to you and build your faith, I pray you will fall more in love with God and his Word. I would love to hear testimonies of what you are learning or even know how I can minister to you, so please visit me at https://www.BethRunkle.com.

Introduction

At times, it felt like brown moving boxes were my decorating scheme. With my husband's fourteen moves while on active duty, moving commotion became normal. In a world of constant change, I found that only faith in an unchanging God could anchor my soul. In the Bible, Sarah and Abraham's lives hold many parallels to the military lifestyle. Abraham and Sarah lived a semi-nomadic lifestyle, traveling from place to place with their livestock from one area of fertile land to another.[1] In the Westernized, modern world, this lifestyle contains several similarities with the military family.

In Genesis 11–12, God called Sarah* and Abraham to leave the land they knew and go to a land God would later identify. God recorded this historical event early in the first book of the

---

* Sarah was called Sarai before God changed her name to Sarah in Genesis 17. God sometimes changed a person's name in the Bible when he was calling that individual to a change in character. Her name change from Sarai to Sarah was when God was calling her to a new season in her relationship with God. For purposes of this study, Sarai will be called Sarah throughout the book.

Bible. This placement articulates for us how God understands and esteems the military spouse.

Sarah and Abraham's move to a location that God would later pinpoint approximates a military Permanent Change of Station (PCS), except they were transporting their household goods on livestock rather than moving trucks. I guess I can no longer complain about our PCSs! By looking at different aspects of Sarah's life, the Word of God will encourage you with the adjustments that come with living the military-wife life.

Your husband likely has a specific calling to serve in the military. The dictionary defines a calling as "a strong inner impulse toward a particular course of action or work which usually involves helping people and may be accompanied by a conviction of divine influence."[2] Did you know that his calling to serve in the military goes beyond just a job or providing for you and any children you may have? It is something for which he feels a strong passion. As my husband's career progressed, I learned to support his calling and embrace the military lifestyle as a joint calling.

But I have my own occupation, unique goals, and giftings in this life, you may be saying to yourself. Do you sometimes feel like you sit in your husband's shadow as he pursues his military career? I've been there! But after twenty-five years in a military marriage, I can say this with certainty: just because your husband's career decides when and where you move, that doesn't mean you cannot embrace your man's military career and lifestyle as a joint venture—and you better believe God will use your unique wiring just as much as he uses your husband's. Accepting your husband's passion as a dual calling will enable you to get behind your man and not just survive the military life but thrive in it!

God chose Sarah to be the mother of his people. In this book, you will see you are also a remarkable woman God sets apart. Your life isn't something that "just happened" to you. Nor is it something God called *only* your husband to. *You, too,* are chosen and called!

Whether you chose it or not, being married to a man serving in uniform has altered your life. Choosing to embrace it will not only bless you, but it will also bless others. Your involvement will also increase your husband's joy in serving and communicate a sincere level of respect.

Have you ever felt like it was a mistake you ended up with a husband who would move all over the world? It's not a misstep. In fact, I believe this is something that God specifically ordained for you. Yep, you're special! In fact, so unique that God chose not to just leave you in your hometown but to grow and mold you as you continually rely on him.

God looks at you and sees the potential of the person you can become as you depend on him more. He wants you to grow into the person he sees. So he selects you to be molded and shaped by the hardships of military life, where you cannot cling to things of this world—but cling only to Christ. God gives us the answers for any situation where we find ourselves. May we seek him before we seek anything else in our lives.

Lingering Loneliness

Genesis 12:1, 4–5; Deuteronomy 31:6

After long-distance dating my husband for two years, he swept me off my feet, but I felt dropped with a thud as we moved three times that first year of marriage. My husband needed to undergo military training en route to his next assignment. As a newlywed, I had no idea the turmoil being an armed forces wife would add to life, nor the extent of loneliness that I would feel. Upon arriving at the operational assignment, my husband deployed for the Middle East within two months. I drowned in emptiness, misery, and sorrow. Has this ever happened to you? I imagine you can relate.

At that time, I didn't know that I would be able to find myself in the pages of the Bible. Genesis 11–12 includes God's call to Abraham and Sarah's life to "go from your land, your relatives, and your father's house to the land that I will show you." As I mentioned in the introduction, his call feels to me like a military Permanent Change of Station (PCS); how about you? Through Abraham, God led Sarah to leave her home and her family and travel to a new land where God reestablished her. Sarah's journey sounds quite similar to a military spouse's journey. Can you imagine her feeling some trepidation?

When it comes to a big move, Sarah may have physically faced even more challenges than a military spouse. Sarah's journey from Haran to Canaan was more than 400 miles and wound along the edge of the barren desert wilderness, traveling along rivers, and would have taken at least three full weeks of constant travel.[1] Sarah would have had to wait many months to begin reestablishing connections in Canaan.

As a military spouse, have you also felt the pain of loneliness when you have to PCS to a new location? You probably also have suffered isolation when your spouse was away on deployment or temporary duty (TDY) orders in another place. Sarah understood loneliness and likely clung to her faith in God for comfort. Sometimes we can be tempted to believe that our faith in God is not enough to sustain us through periods of loneliness, but let me encourage you that not only is it enough, it is also your lifeline!

The name of God used here in Genesis in the original Hebrew language is *El Shaddai*, which translates as the "God Almighty" or "the God who is all-sufficient."[2] If God is mighty and all-sufficient, then he is enough. He can sustain you through periods of isolation. And as strange as it sounds, the Lord may even be ordaining a period of aloneness, so you will rely on him and cling to him more. God may want you to embrace an environment where you feel alone—not to punish you—but so he might prove to you that he is with you and will support you. Think about it: we all want proof that God is near, that God cares, that God will sustain us. But we often miss it because we spend all our energy looking at the people around us instead of upward toward him. Sometimes lonely seasons—seasons where there's not many people to look *around* at—force us to look *up*, where we can finally see God.

Did you know that God doesn't need you or me? He was perfectly happy and content in himself—Father, Son, and Spirit. Which means he created us not because he needed companionship or love (these things were already overflowing within him), but simply because he *wanted* to create us. Said another way, God simply created humanity to be in a relationship with him. If that's the case, he may be allowing a season of loneliness so you will grow in your connection with him. If you respond to him, your isolation can give you the extra time you need to invest in your personal relationship with the Lord. After all, each of us has a deep longing within us that only God can fill. Think of it like a loving parent clearing their child's calendar for the day, so that they can enjoy some needed parent-child time, away from all distractions. Is it unloving for a parent to clear their child's calendar for a short stint? Not at all. It's a sign of desire and love—if only the child will show up to the day with excitement and trust.

If God is all-sufficient, then he is enough, even in our loneliness. We may be magnifying the loneliness by focusing on the negative, isolated feelings more than the joy of the Lord. The key to changing your feelings is to reject this drift to isolation with prayer and an awareness that lingering in your loneliness will only breed more separation.

God's enemy, Satan, loves to feed us lies when we are down. Recognize that he may be serving you lies, which may increase the intensity of your isolation. Memorizing and meditating on Scripture can help you replace the lies that Satan may be feeding you with the truth. When we have Scripture committed to memory, it is easier for the Holy Spirit to bring to mind those previously memorized verses to combat false thoughts. It can also be helpful to turn on some worship music to remind you of the Lord and his presence. Force yourself to get out of your temporary lodging or new housing and engage with others or just go out for some personal exercise (or a stroll with the kids). Remember: being in a season of loneliness doesn't mean you intentionally cut yourself off from human connection. Rather, while you're focusing primarily on investing in your relationship with the Lord, you also make time to go out into the world and build healthy relationships with others.

God himself is with you and can bring comfort and hope to even your darkest days. God's Word says: "I will never leave you or abandon you" (Heb. 13:5). You are his beloved child; you are never alone. Jesus himself understands your loneliness. All his friends and family abandoned him when he stood trial before the religious and Roman authorities. Do you realize he not only sees you in your loneliness, but *understands* it firsthand? Lean into the Lord in your despair and loneliness instead of leaning away from him. God is there, even when no one else is. And remember: he's a God who gets it.

REFLECTION

How can you focus more on the presence of God in times of loneliness?

How can you meet new people or form community with other Christians who can point you to God?

PRAYER

God Almighty, please empower me to lean into you in my loneliness. Help me to be satisfied with you and feel your presence here with me. As I focus on you in this season, bring the right people into my life to satisfy my need for human connection. Give me eyes to see someone else feeling isolated to whom I can connect.

Day
2

Stick like Glue

Genesis 12:1–5; 2:24

In the old sitcom *Everybody Loves Raymond*, most episodes contain a scene in the kitchen where Raymond's overbearing and insulting mother, Marie, embarrassingly forces her views and opinions on Raymond's wife, Debra. The show provides excellent comic relief, but can you imagine living in that household? Well, if you are a military spouse, chances are you will never find yourself living across the street from your in-laws!

One of the most challenging parts of a military family's journey is that we must leave our family and hometown and start over in a new location, usually quite far from those we love. Sarah set an example of how to complete a PCS move successfully. I find it comforting to think that military wives are not the only ones God has called to leave their home and their family and resettle.

Do you often feel lonely and frustrated with the forced relo-
cations during the first days or weeks after arriving at your new
duty location? Amid the challenging parts of being a military
wife, some unique blessings result from this lifestyle. God called
us in Genesis 2:24 to leave our family—our father and mother—
and be united or "cleave" to our spouse. God designed that a husband and wife find their primary human relationship with each
other; this should be a priority over even a parent-child relationship. Can you see how a military marriage can have its blessings
as well as its challenges? Our military marriage can also be a
blessing as circumstances force us to cleave to our spouse because
we live hundreds of miles away from our friends and family. The
Hebrew word translated as "bonds" or "cleave" in Genesis 2:24
refers to "pursuing hard" after something or "being glued to" or
"holding fast" to something.[1]

The "holding fast" definition can be better understood
through welding.[2] Holding fast describes the point where two
pieces of steel are welded together. The iron or steel is heated
and melted until the molecules are forced together into one
continuous piece.[3] Surprisingly, if the right metals are used and
the appropriate heat is applied, the resulting material is actually
stronger at the weld.[4]

So when we correctly cleave to our husbands, we become
much stronger than either of us could be on our own. It may take
some heat to develop the right level of strength, but the result is
something stronger than the two separate pieces. The military
lifestyle might be part of the heat being applied to your marriage

to make your weld, or bond, stronger. Don't let Satan trick you into thinking that the heat can weaken you instead of making you stronger.

Forced resettling comes with the military life, and it causes us to often find ourselves more drawn to our spouse as we brave a brand-new location with no one familiar but our husbands. The forced separation from family also causes military spouses to rely on one another more than if parents and in-laws were right down the street. With a fresh perspective, you can set up a house with your spouse in a new town. You can begin a family or new career with unique ideas and routines. You can establish new traditions. All without as much friction or pushback that typically comes with having family nearby!

Right after God made a woman from man, Scripture makes it clear that an important pattern for marriage is set forth: for the couple to leave their parents and stick like glue to one another (Gen. 2:21-24). God knows we will fail to be in harmony and genuinely united with our spouse if we don't "unglue" ourselves from our parents. Today, you and I need to mourn certain parts of being separated from family, no doubt, but we can simultaneously choose to be thankful for the excellent opportunity for unity that it can provide in marriage.

God also designed the leaving and cleaving in marriage to be a picture of the intimate relationship he wants with you. The same Hebrew word for "cleave" is used in Deuteronomy 13:4 and 30:20 when God commanded the Israelites to be faithful to him.

Although I'm challenging you to prioritize and bond to your spouse, I am not suggesting you should never talk to your family or in-laws. With your warrior away serving his country often, you may be the connection point to his family at times. Boundaries are important, but I am not advocating you completely cut anyone out of your lives unless there are exceptional reasons.

Some tips to help you and your husband "leave and cleave" better:

- Give your spouse priority over parents, siblings, and even children by reordering your priority list to be God, spouse, and then others.
- When facing a decision, determine to consult one another's counsel first before going to outside counsel.
- As much as possible, avoid involving the extended family in any marital conflict to prevent unintentionally tainting your spouse's reputation with your family. (This does not mean you should be facing conflicts alone when you truly need a third party; rather, choose a third party who is as unbiased as possible, like a Christian counselor.)
- Trust God to be the "cleaving glue." When there doesn't seem to be anything to cling to

in your marriage, cling to God himself and remain committed to your marriage and to the Lord.

- Recognize that cleaving is a choice. Don't give yourself any other option but to cleave. Take the word *divorce* off the table, and never use it as a threat during a fight, so that you aren't tempted to think it is a viable option (apart from abuse, which would make it prudent).

REFLECTION

Are you prioritizing your marriage relationship and sticking like glue to your spouse?

How can you better show unity to your spouse and separate from your parents?

PRAYER

Loving God, help me to prioritize my marriage above all other relationships. Help my husband and me to cling to one another. Give us a fresh perspective on the blessing of moving away from family.

Day
3

Being an Influencer

Genesis 12:6–9

One year, we temporarily landed in two different states for training before moving on to my husband's next assignment. Two years later, the military forced us to move again with another training en route. So in three years, we lived temporarily in six locations! Although we weren't moving around on camels or donkeys, I can relate to Sarah's transient lifestyle. Do you often wonder if moving is your hobby?

At the beginning of Sarah and Abraham's journey, we see the first stops in their nomadic and unsettled lifestyle. God chose to take them from one part of the ancient world to another. God chose Abraham and Sarah to be the special ones to take God's revelation of himself to the world. Perhaps this was because they were traveling from place to place with a potential for impacting

the most people—especially since Canaan was along the most traveled trade route of the ancient world.[1] At this time in history, most
ancient cultures worshipped local deities. When they moved to a
new location, people often left that deity behind and worshipped
the new god in the new place.[2] God called Sarah and Abraham to
leave behind the false god they had previously worshipped, but he
also called them to continue revering him as they moved around.

Sarah and Abraham took servants with them on their journey
who would have watched them worship differently than all the
cultures around them. In Genesis 12:7, we see that the first thing
Abraham and Sarah did upon arriving in Canaan was to present
an offering to the Lord. God didn't require this, but Abraham
was compelled to offer praise and thanksgiving to the Lord for
bringing them to this fertile, lush land. Those who saw Sarah and
Abraham worship may have asked questions about their exclusive
God. We have evidence in Genesis 24:12–14, 26–27 that at least
one of Abraham's servants worshipped and prayed to God.

Since the ancient culture worshipped pagan gods distinct to
each location, moving to follow a deity would have been revolu-
tionary for Sarah and Abraham. Following a god from one place
to another was highly unusual since their gods were bound by
location. Because continuing to worship a deity from one location
to another was so different from the pagan religions of their time,
Sarah likely would have understood how profound their decision
was. It's possible that she saw the importance of her role as the
mother of a new nation who would worship one singular God and
eventually reveal him to the world.

Genesis 14 tells us that Abraham had a fighting force of more than three hundred men. Throughout history, God has used military members to move his individuals to locations where they can impact more souls with the good news. Roman guards and soldiers who heard about Jesus's life, death, and resurrection from many of the Christians they had imprisoned partially helped disperse the message of Jesus in the years following his ascension. The Anglo-Saxons also shared the news of Jesus as they invaded and conquered European territory.[3]

Military families can be a powerful mechanism to reach the world with the message of Christ—not by the strength of the armed forces, but by the power of the gospel (Rom. 1:16)! You, too, are called to be an influencer as you transplant. How does that feel to think that the Lord might have a special purpose for you to influence other men, women, and families as you move around? In each location, no matter how long or short you live there, choose to take a bold stance for Christ and influence those around you. Other military members and families need the confidence to know that a sovereign God controls their lives, including where they PCS and are sent on deployment. You are called to this transient lifestyle and the opportunity to influence more people with the hope of Christ. I've wasted opportunities before. Don't waste this opportunity to be the messenger of hope to a fellow military spouse or neighbor.

You can live on mission to reach the lost people whom God has put in front of you. I believe all military families are just like missionaries—they can take the gospel with them as they move around. Who are the people who don't know the Lord on your base, in your housing area, or in your regular gatherings? Get into the mess of the lives of those around you. Love them in the name of Jesus and arm yourself with the truth and love of the gospel.

Unfortunately, both the Christians and Muslims fighting in the Crusades were known to make converts, often using military strength. I'd never advocate for anyone to use force to convert. But while on duty with the military, you can take the opportunity to openly share the gospel and invite others to make their own free choice to become a follower of Christ.

REFLECTION

How can you be an influencer for Christ to those with whom you interact in the military community? Is there anything you need to take off your plate so you can make space for this?

Where are you stationed right now? How can you intentionally invest in others spiritually right now, in that place?

PRAYER

Strong Tower, help me to take a bold stance for Christ so that I genuinely leave an imprint on others with the good news of Jesus in each location we encounter. Give me eyes to see those around me who need to know about the life-giving Lord.

Life-Giving Counterpart

Genesis 12:10–20; Ephesians 5:22–23

My friend and her husband would soon move to a new location for military orders. On a house-hunting trip, they found few home choices, on base and off, and eventually signed a contract for a new-build home. My friend did not want to build; she knew the work would be difficult with her husband deploying and his lack of "handyman" skills. After politely making her desires known to her husband, she went along with his decision to build with an offer for the home to be contingent on the sale of their home in the last duty station. She told God about her reluctance to build and willingness to submit to her husband even though she disagreed.

Wouldn't you know it? God orchestrated the details perfectly—the home they currently owned did not sell in the contingency period. The lack of contingency sale resulted in them renting a house for six months and then finding the exact model of home they had selected with the builder, already complete with upgrades without the extra cost or hassle. God honored her obedience to submit with abundant blessings. Have you had a similar situation where you trusted God to protect you from what you perceived as a poor decision on the part of your husband? Or have you not trusted God with one of your husband's decisions? I admit I've done the latter much more frequently than I should have.

The term *submission* gets a bad rap in the twenty-first century and is often far from biblical submission. When God made Adam and Eve, God called Eve a helper corresponding to him (Gen. 2:18). The Hebrew term for "helper" means "life-giving counterpart."[1] The role of the wife is by no means lesser. God doesn't view the woman in a subservient role to the man. A woman is a helper, but so is God. God uses the Hebrew word for "helper" in Genesis 2:18, regarding Eve's role, to refer to himself. The same term is applied sixty-six times in the Bible, referring to God and his strength, power, protection, and being a rescuer.[2] Further, in the New Testament, Jesus describes the Holy Spirit as a helper (John 14:16, 26; 15:26; 16:7). This Holy Spirit is coequal with God the Father and God the Son.

So submission is not being a doormat but trusting the God-ordained family order. How do we submit to our husbands? The biblical way is to respectfully share opinions and mutual respect through an organizational structure that provides resolution for difficult decisions (instead of allowing disagreements to continue indefinitely). This orderly structure helps a husband and wife live together in peace.

As Paul states in Ephesians 5:23, the roles of husband and wife are assigned so that the observing world would see a picture of Christ and the church. Man and wife together are to be an earthly metaphor for the gospel. Paul said "this mystery is profound" in Ephesians 5:32, pointing to Genesis 2:24 and implying that the concept of marriage is the mystery that is ultimately about the union between Christ and his church.[3] Our marriage is supposed to be a living picture of God's love that was given to us through Jesus. The roles given to husband and wife are embedded in the distinctive roles of Christ and his church.[4] Husband and wife each have a part to play. The husband is to love his wife with a sacrificial love. The husband puts his wife's needs above his own, like the love Christ has for the church. Wives are to be subject to their husband because the church follows the head or authority of it, Christ.

Since there was a famine in the land, Abraham and Sarah fled to the fertile soil of Egypt, where crops could still grow. The Scriptures tell us that Sarah was exceedingly attractive, so much so that Abraham feared the pharaoh of Egypt would want her badly enough to murder her husband. So Abraham conveyed that he and Sarah were siblings to save his own neck. Read it for yourself:

> When [Abraham] was about to enter Egypt, he
> said to his wife, Sarai, "Look, I know what a
> beautiful woman you are. When the Egyptians

> see you, they will say, 'This is his wife.' They
> will kill me but let you live. Please say you're my
> sister so it will go well for me because of you,
> and my life will be spared on your account."
> (Gen. 12:11–13)

Here's the thing: Abraham wasn't technically lying, as he and Sarah were indeed half-siblings (back then, marriage customs were quite different). But it is clear that he made no mention of her being his wife. I imagine Sarah may not have fully trusted Abraham's scheme. Knowing Pharaoh might take her into his harem, can you imagine how Sarah felt? Living in an ancient-culture harem sounds a bit like the popular TV show *The Bachelor*, only worse, as there would have been more women in this harem than in the cast of *The Bachelor*—and who knows how many against their will. Surprisingly, Sarah agreed to follow Abraham's decision. First Peter 3:5–6 tells us that Sarah is commended for her faith because she obeyed Abraham and did not give way to fear. While I'm not recommending that you join a harem at the whim of your husband (the everyday choices we face in marriage are much different now than they were then), the general point is that if our God is sovereign, he is able to protect us and provide for us even in the midst of what seems to be an unwise decision of our husband.

Absolutely, I need to give my husband my input, but then I need to submit to my husband in whatever final direction or resolution he offers our family. My assurance is not in my husband, but in God, and if I submit to God's order of things, then I know

God can protect me even if my husband makes a bad choice. I might not always agree with my husband's decisions, but I can always trust a God who can divinely orchestrate the details, even if my husband makes a poor choice.*

Interestingly, God did indeed protect Abraham and Sarah. While Abraham's plan worked and even seemed to prosper Abraham's family for a short time (Gen. 12:14–16), eventually, Pharaoh found out Abraham was lying to him, and justice was served. By whom, you ask? God himself. Here's how the Bible puts it:

> But the LORD struck Pharaoh and his household with severe plagues because of Abram's wife, Sarai. So Pharaoh sent for Abram and said, "What have you done to me? Why didn't you tell me she was your wife? Why did you say, 'She's my sister,' so that I took her as my wife? Now, here is your wife. Take her and go!" Then Pharaoh gave his men orders about him, and they sent him away with his wife and all he had. (Gen. 12:17–20)

Who struck Pharoah for taking a wife that did not belong to him? Who freed Sarah from an illegitimate marriage, orchestrated by her own husband? *The Lord!* God's sovereignty means

---

* Submission to a husband does not mean a wife would submit to her husband in an area that would cause her harm or cause her to sin. That would be going against the will of God. If your husband is asking you to do anything that would harm you or sin, please seek professional help.

that he is able to protect us, both in our husband's good decisions and bad ones!

(P.S.: While this particular situation of Abraham and Sarah's life reveals a husband's wrong choice, there are plenty of examples when Abraham made a good choice—a choice that inevitably blessed his family. While you may disagree with your husband on some of his choices, remember to look out for all the other times you followed his lead and it turned out to be the right course of action! God is just as present and protective in those seasons too!)

REFLECTION

What about being a military wife makes submission harder?

Can you recall a time when God honored your submission to your husband? How does that past memory give you faith and courage for today?

PRAYER

Sovereign One, give me the courage to offer honest input to my husband when a big decision comes our way, and the strength to yield to the direction he chooses in the end. Help me remember you can orchestrate decisions for my good and your glory, even when I might disagree with my husband's choice. Help me remember you, O Lord, can even work amid conclusions I might not understand.

Tent-Dwellers

Genesis 12:1–9; Matthew 6:19–20

I tried to like tent camping. Camping is the only vacation where you work harder preparing meals and caring for your living space than at home. I'd spend an entire day packing all the stuff for the camping trip and another unpacking. I think God called me to do more than just occasional tent camping because he planned for me to be a tent-dweller. So, instead of tent camping, our mode of operation was just to move all of our household belongings, on average, every 1.7 years. I know it's a crazy way to travel! God knew I tended to cling to things of this world, so every year or two, God orchestrated my husband's orders to cause us to move not just a small tent full of things but an entire household of belongings and pick up and move our lives and our relationships. God wanted me to adhere only to him.

27

At Babel (Gen. 11:1–9), God confused the people's language to keep them from building a permanent foundation that would cause them to rely more upon themselves and less upon God.[1] God beckoned Abraham shortly after the Tower of Babel incident. This placement is essential to understanding God's purposes for the military family. The Babel people were seeking independence and sufficiency apart from God.[2] The next biblical story after Babel is the account of Sarah and Abraham. With them, we see God causing the new family of God to travel and constantly be on the move, living in tents. The Father does this because he knows man will forget his need for God.[3]

Abraham is unique because God called him to leave his land and his people in pagan culture to follow and worship him. The idea of a Yahweh worshipper was totally foreign to their culture. Then God called him to be a tent-dweller for the rest of his life.

Abraham followed God and left everything behind. I know it has probably been hard for you to leave your family and head off to the unknown land where the military was sending you. It was even more challenging for Sarah. Everything in the ancient family structure was centered around the father and financially tied to his trade and legacy.[4] Abraham and Sarah's identity would have been wrapped up in the identity of Terah, Abraham's father. Leaving one's family would have resulted in a response as profound as when the prodigal son left his father in Luke 15.[5] So Abraham and Sarah left behind their paycheck, their pagan god(s), their inheritance, their family, and even their decision-making model. They laid it all on the line to follow God.

When Abraham arrived in the Promised Land after a journey of more than 400 miles, Yahweh appeared to Abraham and reminded him that he would grant him the land (Gen. 12:7). In the Tower of Babel incident, the people had built a tower to glorify themselves. In verse 7, instead of building a tower to himself, Abraham built an altar to the Lord. Think about that: Abraham, who would continue to live in tents for the rest of his life, built something permanent for God. Abraham seems to acknowledge that God's promises and name are the only things that can be permanent. Abraham and Sarah had to be mobile themselves to see their need for and dependence upon God. God wanted them—and you and me—to keep moving and following his voice.

In the same way that God called Sarah and Abraham to be mobile—to keep moving and following his voice—he is calling you as a military wife to passionately pursue him. You have an invitation to intimacy with God as you follow your man in the mobile life caused by the military. The Lord is calling you to see your desperate need for him and your dependence upon him. Where others might dig in their heels and build a tower to themselves, you can go where God sends you, offering your life as a living sacrifice on his altar (Rom. 12:1–2), and remembering that he is the only permanent thing in this life.

I know this may be a challenging perspective change, especially if you are looking at your high school friends who still are best friends and hang out with each other and their children. Pause and consider: this opportunity is a blessing! Every time you think about your next PCS or how you'll be living out of a suitcase and sleeping on a blow-up bed, resist the groan. Stop and remind yourself: God has ordained this "tent-dweller life" because it is his call to you to cling to him. You are to build as you go, but you are not building things that will perish and burn up; you are building a lifestyle that will depend daily on the Lord and be consecrated to him—this is heavenly treasure.

REFLECTION

What has been the most challenging part about leaving home and family?

How can you keep your perspective focused on the special and unique call you have to rely upon the permanence of God amid temporary dwellings and surroundings?

PRAYER

My true Treasure, help me focus on the priceless heavenly treasure I have in you. Help me to remember you are to be the only permanent thing in my life. Enable me to resist the temptation to cling to things of this world.

Day
6

Set-Apart Lives

Genesis 12:6–8; 13; 18–19

My husband had the privilege and thrill of flying a fighter aircraft during part of his Air Force career. He loved the risk and adventure; I tried not to think about the daily danger he faced. It might not be a healthy coping mechanism, but I often pretended he had a typical office job like other husbands. Interestingly, during a deployment to Saudi Arabia, my husband began to have spiritual conversations with fellow fighter pilots. God used those conversations to open my husband's eyes to his sinful condition and need for a Savior.

The fighter pilot community worked hard and played hard. During this deployment, my husband noticed two guys in his squadron that continued to live lives that stood out as distinctively different. They were excellent pilots, personable, and even "cool," yet avoided any immoral behavior surrounding them and kept their mouths clean. My husband noticed they were distinctive and began a conversation with them about how they could continue to resist temptation. This conversation led to further discussions about the Christian faith, which catalyzed him becoming a believer.

As I mentioned in Day 3, the first thing Sarah and Abraham did upon arriving in Canaan's lavish land was set up an altar and worship God. They thanked God for all he had given them and for keeping his promise to take them to the Promised Land. Abraham did not worship God secretly or privately but "called on the name of the LORD" (Gen. 12:8). Calling on the Lord indicates less than subtle worship and might have even called attention to his reverence of a singular God.[1] Abraham and Sarah did not worry about what those around them were doing or fear people's disapproval of their different worship practices. When everyone around them worshipped pagan gods in elaborate temple ceremonies, Abraham and Sarah chose to honor God and live differently.

Through studying the account of Abraham and his nephew Lot splitting the land, we learn that Abraham appeared to have made choices that caused him to be distinctively dissimilar from Lot and the Canaanites living around him. As described in Genesis 13, Abraham and his nephew Lot had so many livestock that the land they had been residing in could no longer support them. So Abraham humbly offered Lot the first opportunity to choose the territory where he would settle. Lot chose the fertile and well-watered land in the plain of the Jordan, which was near Sodom. Lot may have made this decision due to the prosperity he envisioned by planting crops on better land. Generously, Abraham allowed his nephew to choose the preferred territory. Lot may have thought he had won a prize.

Interestingly, God abundantly blessed Abraham even though he had done what others might not have thought wise by giving his younger nephew the first choice. Culturally, in their time, Abraham should have had the first selection as the elder of the two. Abraham happily let Lot have the better land and followed the Lord to the trees of Mamre, near Hebron (Gen. 13:18), where he immediately built an altar to the Lord. Once again, Abraham chose to worship and honor God no matter what those around him were doing or what expectations they held.

Later in Genesis 18–19, we see that God decreed the destruction of Lot's land and wealth because the "outcry against Sodom and Gomorrah is immense, and their sin is extremely serious . . . the outcry against its people is so great before the Lord" (Gen. 18:20; 19:13). God saved Lot and his immediate family, but only because God "remembered Abraham and brought Lot out of the middle of the upheaval" before God poured out judgment on the wickedness of the inhabitants of this city (Gen. 19:29).

Since Scripture mentions Lot sitting in the gateway of the city in Genesis 19:1, we know that Lot likely served as part of the city's ruling council.[2] If he was indeed serving in leadership, this means the townspeople likely accepted him. He would not have been considered an outsider to the citizens but an active

participant. While it's certainly not wrong for one of God's followers to have leadership roles in their local community—and the
Bible does tell us to live among outsiders in a way that amasses a
good reputation (1 Tim. 3:7; Prov. 22:1; Eccles. 7:1; 1 Pet. 2:12)—
we have to wonder why, after so many years there, Lot's influence
did not yield even ten converts to the faith (Gen. 18:22–33). If it
had, God would have spared the whole city, but he didn't!

Did Lot so want to be accepted by the townsfolk that he
compromised in order to go along with their wicked ways? Did
he overlook some of the immoral and evil activities? Did he seek
to be not just in the world but *of* the world? Regardless of the
details, this much is clear: every bit of wealth and comfort Lot
had in this world was destroyed when God executed judgment on
Sodom and Gomorrah. The evil of the city around him may not
have cost him his life, but it caused Lot to lose all his livestock,
crops, home, and even his wife (see Gen. 19 and Day 25). Could
Lot have spoken out about the immorality he saw and possibly
spared thousands of people from death? Could he have better
used his position of influence to bring others to know God? We'll
never know.

One thing we do know is this: God blessed and provided for
Abraham because he had chosen to live a life not necessarily separated from a certain city (for all cities have sin in them!), but certainly a life separated from evil in terms of his heart and behavior.
Even while dwelling in a pagan city, he chose the ways of Yahweh
instead of the ways of the world. Living in a military culture, you
will likely be surrounded by unwholesome influences. You will

be challenged to live in the world but not be of the world (John 17:14). You can influence them for good instead of being dragged down into the sin around you. While living a life set apart for the Lord can be difficult, it is always worthwhile and its distinctiveness may draw others to faith in Christ.

REFLECTION

In what ways does your life look more like the world than separate from it?

What is one thing you can do this week to live a set-apart and holy life while living in the military community? Consider what this looks like alongside God's call to draw near to lost people who don't know God.

PRAYER

Prince of Peace, awaken me to where I am looking too much like the world around me. Empower me by your Holy Spirit to live a distinctive life for you that will be noticed by others—not for my glory but as an opportunity to draw others to a saving relationship with Christ.

(Day
7)

Where's Your Focus?

Genesis 12:10–20; James 1:5

In 1999, a group of psychologists conducted a study where they asked participants to watch a video of individuals passing basketballs between them and count the passes among players dressed in white while ignoring those passing wearing black. The participants didn't notice a person in a black gorilla suit walking in and out of the scene, thumping his chest. This study showed that individuals could focus so intently on something that they become blind to what is happening right in front of them.[1] We, too, can do something similar when we concentrate too attentively on our circumstances and not on our God.

Famine was a periodic occurrence in biblical times and was often used by God as a disciplinary test. Usually, many Middle Easterners fled to Egypt's Nile River, where the annual flooding of the waters would ensure fertile soil and, therefore, food. In Abraham's life, this was a test to see if Abraham would rely upon his own arm of flesh or the arm of God.[2] James 1:5 instructs us: "if any of you lacks wisdom, he should ask God—who gives to all generously." There is no record that Abraham asked God's advice before he departed for Egypt.[3] Had Abraham consulted God, perhaps he could have avoided many of the difficulties that came about as a result of his time in Egypt.[4]

Since God had promised to bless Abraham and make him into a great nation, God had to sustain Abraham and his family to fulfill his promise. God sustained other biblical characters; he fed the Israelites with manna throughout Exodus (Exod. 16), nourished Elijah with the ravens (1 Kings 17:6), and then provided again through the widow's multiplying oil and flour (1 Kings 17:14). It seems that Abraham trusted God for his eternal interest but was afraid to trust God to supply his temporal needs.[5] Had Abraham waited and asked the Lord, he might have avoided the many problems that came to him in Egypt.[6] Abraham had lost his peace and feeling of security. Abraham and Sarah were likely focused too intently on the circumstances and not on their God. So Abraham took matters into his own hands and put the weight of his future on his own shoulders.

When Abraham worried about his own safety, he risked his wife's safety. His lack of faith led to his selfishness. Temporarily, Abraham turned away from God and began to center everything on himself.[7] Perhaps Abraham was looking at what everyone else around him was doing when a physical challenge presented itself.

It seems Abraham's circumstances caused him to doubt the size of his God.

As we saw in Day 4, God displayed his love for Sarah when he showed up to rescue her from Pharaoh's harem. God exhibited how he could be trusted to keep his word. God had made promises to Sarah and Abraham, so God was faithful to protect them.[8]

Amazingly, God was not frustrated or defeated by Abraham's failure. God intervened to bring a plague on Pharaoh's household which caused Pharaoh to rebuke Abraham and send him and Sarah away. Even though Abraham had been unfaithful at this point, God remained faithful and brought Sarah and Abraham safely back to himself.[9] This account shows that God is willing to use ordinary, imperfect men and women to accomplish his will. Abraham slipped, but God drew him back. Even though Abraham had lapsed in faith, he returned to God and was responsive to his leading.

As a wife of a man serving in arms, situations will inevitably be out of your control. You may find that PCS or deployment orders will tempt you to question God's sovereignty. Your famine-like situation may be your husband's safety. Or perhaps the particulars of your husband's promotion timing or manner might add to your fear or uncertainty. Remember, God is Lord of your eternal and also of your temporal. He can be trusted. He can see things you cannot. His status as Creator means he is not bound by time and exists outside of time. Adjust your glasses and see the God who dwarfs and outpowers your circumstances. Resist the temptation to intervene on every little detail of your husband's career, his next move, or his deployment. God doesn't need you to intervene. Why? Because while your input matters, the weight of those things is not ultimately on your shoulders. It is on God's.

REFLECTION

When are you most tempted to take matters into your own hands?

When you face frustrating situations, do you pray to God, or run to someone else first? Why?

PRAYER

I confess, Everlasting Father, I don't always rely upon you and maintain peace when circumstances swirl around me. Help me to remember you are an eternal God, but you also hold the temporal in your hand. Aid me in passing the test of faith and trusting you when physical challenges approach me. Keep me from trying to flex my own arms of strength but to turn to you for guidance, counsel, and peace because your arms are limitless and trustworthy.

Climb on the Altar

Genesis 13:1–4; Romans 12:1–2

The movie *Top Gun* portrayed fighter pilots with an appetite for danger and an enormous ego. Maverick mocked rules and broke rules of engagement and still succeeded in his military career, demonstrating it was pure fiction. With iconic scenes like the buzzing of the tower, Maverick and Goose feeling the need for speed, and Iceman and Maverick bickering in the locker room, the movie drew the audience into the conflict. Although it made for a compelling film, Iceman and Maverick's push for perfection and desire to beat one another at all costs taught us about worship. Worship? Yes, worship. Tim Keller succinctly says, "You don't get to decide to worship. Everyone worships something."[1] We get to decide what we will worship. Even atheists worship something. Maverick and Iceman spent all their time, thoughts, and energy trying to finish in the top spot in training and showed they worshipped only themselves.

After Abraham failed in Egypt, he and Sarah returned to Canaan and went straight to the spot where he had first worshipped God in Bethel. The journey to and from Egypt was lost time for Sarah and Abraham. Perhaps Abraham hung his head in shame during the return trip because he had lost faith in God. Abraham didn't stay defeated once he returned; he immediately got to work on worship. Abraham's time in Egypt without building an altar is an indication that he lacked fellowship with God.[2] After God rescued Sarah from Abraham's selfish choice and lack of trust in God, Sarah and Abraham returned to God and worshipped him rather than themselves.

Abraham's choices in Egypt may have tempted Sarah to tell Abraham, "I told you so," but she worshipped the Lord instead. Imagine Sarah dancing before the Lord in worship as she realized how merciful God had been by allowing her to escape Pharaoh's harem. God plucked Sarah out of the harem where she would have been deprived of both love and value. On top of that, she still received the promise of eventually bearing a son that would be an ancestor to the Messiah. Sarah now had a practical picture of the protection and provision of God. I imagine Sarah graciously supported Abraham in their family's worship of the one true God.

Old Testament sacrifices consisted of a burnt offering of an animal placed on the altar and entirely consumed by the flames (Lev. 1:9). This sacrifice atoned for the one who offered it. In biblical times, this was costly for the worshipper and represented trusting in God for provision for the future. God may have given this example because he wants us to offer up our lives to be consumed for God, yet ever living.[3] Romans 12:1 helps explain the Old Testament's sacrificial meaning by urging us to present our bodies as a living sacrifice as an act of worship. Instead of asking for death, God asks that we live each moment as an act of worship to God. So, worship isn't just what happens in church on Sunday morning or when you turn on music on the radio. It's how you live your life each day.

Worship involves obedience, but it isn't something we can do in our own strength. We do it once we respond to God's saving grace and mercy in accepting Jesus's sacrifice on our behalf. We respond obediently by dying to ourselves and living sacrificially for the Lord. We want to obey God. We are not doing it to win God's acceptability; Jesus has already won our right standing with God on our behalf. Jesus is asking for more than your heart; he is asking for you to give all of yourself to him in response to the fact that he gave all of himself for you.

Worshipping God involves living for God, obeying God, delighting in God's Word, and living out his Word. God sincerely wants you to climb on the altar of sacrifice and offer yourself there each day. But being on the altar requires us to re-evaluate our position continually, recognize when we've slid off the altar, and climb back up there. If you're like me, you slide off the altar regularly.

Being a living sacrifice involves resisting conforming to the world, which means the culture around you does not rule you. Our standard cannot be what those around us are doing; our bar should be what God calls us to do. We become attuned to our position off the altar by regularly renewing our minds by being in the Word. Time in the Word gives us the energy to climb back on that altar and do so joyfully.

Are you worshipping God, self, or something else? Plenty of good things still don't deserve the time and attention we give them. Only God is worthy of true worship.

One thing I struggled to worship was the illusion of control I held in my life. Sure, with a husband serving in the military, much of my life was out of my control, but I struggled to try to control every detail I possibly could. I was telling myself and others I was just a good planner. But, in reality, I was worshipping myself—my own self-sufficiency. When I relied upon myself, I wasn't trusting the sovereignty of God and his presence. I had to repent of placing myself on the altar and learn to surrender control of my life to God—sometimes daily!

Another object of my worship was worshipping my identity. Truth is, if our identity is grounded in anything but Christ, we will be disappointed. When I first married my husband, I struggled with feelings of inadequacy because before following him around the world, my identity had been tied to my position at work and my abilities and achievements. In my new role, I constantly felt as if I didn't measure up. Some wives can also place their identity in their husband's role or rank—that's too much pressure for him. An identity secured in God and who he says we are allows us to walk in freedom. It was helpful for me to keep a running list of who God said I was posted in my home to remind myself of my identity in Christ. I also tucked a copy of the list in my Bible so that I could refer to it when I was struggling to plant my identity in who Christ says I am. Below is a short list of who God says I am. In Christ, I am:

- God's child (John 1:12)
- A friend of Jesus Christ (John 15:15)
- God's workmanship (Eph. 2:10)
- Chosen (Eph. 1:4)
- Free from condemnation (Rom. 8:1–2)
- Not given a spirit of fear but of power, love, and a sound judgment (2 Tim. 1:7)
- Bought with a price and I belong to God (1 Cor. 6:19–20)
- A person with direct access to the throne of grace through Jesus Christ (Heb. 4:14–16)
- Born of God and the evil one cannot touch me (1 John 5:18)

REFLECTION

What are you worshipping? What occupies your thoughts? What do you spend most of your time doing?

How can you more quickly recognize when you've slid off the altar?

PRAYER

I confess, True God, that sometimes I slide off the altar, and other times I consciously climb down. Help me climb back on the altar and return there quickly each time I lose my position. Thank you that because of Jesus, I am forgiven. Help me get off the throne of my own life by surrendering my ambitions to you and your purposes. I want to live a life of worship, which means I surrender to your will for where we live and the amount of time my husband can be at home. Assist me in sacrificially representing you in the military community and the places you have us temporarily call home.

Peace over Possessions

Genesis 13:5–10; Psalm 1:1; Luke 12:15

We lived on a military installation several times. Although the government provided all we needed, the homes we occupied in installation housing didn't have the latest modern conveniences. Our homes were basic and simple. One of the last places we lived included replacement cabinet doors in the kitchen made out of unstained plywood. Fancy, huh?

When we lived on base, we formed closer connections with military families because those were our neighbors and playmates for my kids. I spent afternoons before dinner and later in the evenings hanging out in the street with my neighbors. As another benefit, it prevented the temptation to play the comparison game with our friends' newest upgrades or additions to their homes. Base or Post families all had identical homes that were nothing special, and all our husbands were in the same pay grade, so our salaries were essentially the same. Another blessing of the military wife's life; it helped prevent some covetousness.

God had sent Abraham, Sarah, and Lot out of Egypt with great wealth, which included much livestock and servants. Since they had so many animals, the land couldn't support them both, and conflict ensued. Since the Bible mentioned the Canaanites and Perizzites dwelling in the land in Genesis 13:7, it is possible that Abraham may have been concerned about how their testimony may have been affecting all the people who were not followers of God.[1] What do your neighbors see when they watch you?

In addition to the effect of his and Lot's behavior, Abraham and Sarah had just learned a valuable lesson in Egypt: they could trust God with every detail of their lives. Abraham was the older male and patriarch of their family unit, so rightfully, he should have had his choice of land. Because Sarah and Abraham had faith in God, they knew they didn't need to assert themselves to have God's best.[2] So they chose to be generous and let Lot have the first choice. Abraham didn't insist on his rights; he chose peace over possessions.[3] We see no evidence that Sarah worked around Abraham to try and get the land that was rightly theirs for the choosing. Perhaps Abraham's recent failure in faith prompted both Sarah and Abraham to leave material things and positions in God's hands.

Lot put on his worldly glasses and focused on the lush, fertile ground of the Jordan plain and the ease of living there in his agrarian culture. Even though the men of Sodom were exceedingly wicked, Lot chose to live near them. Although we don't know Lot's motive, it's possible he took advantage of his uncle's generosity and served himself with the best land. Early church fathers Chrysostom and Ambrose interpreted Lot's choice as presumptuous or motivated by selfishness and greed.[4] Even though we don't definitively know his rationale, we see no evidence that Lot sought the Lord's direction. He did choose, unwisely, to live near and sit in government with the mockers. The prospect of power in Sodom may have tempted Lot's pride. Lot may have coveted the wealth and ease of his potential neighbors and wanted the best land at Abraham's expense.

We see a contrast here between Abraham's generosity and preference for others and Lot's choice to take the best "for himself" (Gen. 13:11). God orchestrated the end result in Abraham's favor. Sarah and Abraham selflessly gave to Lot, but God allowed them abundant blessings anyway. As we'll see later, Lot drew ever-closer to evil over the course of time. Abraham's testimony became greater because he was willing to trust God and be content with what God gave him.

Coveting is when we yearn to possess something someone else has. We can covet material possessions, but we can also covet others' lives. A military wife can be tempted to covet a position or promotion for her husband. She can also selfishly desire the family life she sees in her neighbors or others in her husband's unit. Comparison kills contentment—so avoid comparison!

A common thing for a military wife to covet is a career she doesn't possess because she follows her husband around during this season of life. It might even be the level of a profession she is able to attain. I'm not saying that a wife shouldn't or couldn't have her own career, but there are seasons when we do so with adjustments so that there's space for our husbands to continue serving in the armed forces.

Social media is also a considerable trap for coveting. Consider your thoughts about the plastic world you see as you scroll. Are you coveting your friends' highlight reels or even feeling left out because you aren't in someone's post or story? What you see is not reality. The images shown in social media are carefully chosen with edited videos and carefully constructed content. Realize you will be affected by what you are viewing. Social media can have a sneaky negative effect on viewers. Stop comparing yourself and thinking you don't measure up. Face-to-face connections will be more fulfilling than social media and likely result in less coveting. Work to intentionally engage in more real-life relationships that can grant you peace.

REFLECTION

What are some of the things, positions, or people you covet? What steps can you take to actively fight against this?

What would generosity and preference for others look like in this season of your life? What would choosing peace over possessions look like?

PRAYER

Gracious God, thank you for all you have given to me. I want to be content with what I have and resist the temptation to covet what I don't. Assist me to view my role as a military wife as significant and not less than others and enable me to trust you to prepare a season for pursuing my goals. I want to intentionally engage in more face-to-face relationships and be generous, deferent, peaceful, willing, and vulnerable.

Day
10

Your Spiritual Weapon

Genesis 14:1–16; Ephesians 6:18

Sitting on the edge of the airfield as the sun peeked its head over the horizon, I watched the red fire of the afterburner light up on the jet that held my husband as he headed off to the Middle East for his first deployment. Tears streamed down my face as I realized he was gone, and it would be months before I saw him again. Watching him leave in a military fighter jet made it painfully clear that my husband was headed off to combat and would encounter danger and possibly even death. I was helpless to protect him. I was an unbeliever and had no one to run to with my fear. Future deployments were somewhat easier because, by that time, I knew I could trust in a sovereign God. But that first deployment was especially challenging.

Do you struggle with the fear of letting your man go into harm's way? While your husband may be off on authentic adventures fighting legitimate battles with the military, you can grab your spiritual weapons and fight for your man.

Abraham "called on the name of the LORD" in Genesis 12:8, 13:4, and 21:33. Abraham did this when he built an altar to God, but this "calling" likely included an audible prayer during which he thanked, praised, worshipped, and petitioned God.[1] Sarah witnessed and might have participated in this sincere prayer. Part of what separated Abraham and Sarah from those around them was their worship of a singular God. Psalm 145:18 tells us that God is near to those who call out to him in prayer.

The Jewish Talmud is second to the Hebrew Bible in Jewish religious tradition. The Talmud records several instances of Sarah petitioning the Sovereign Lord and placing her absolute trust in him.[2] The Bible illustrates Sarah's faith by recording her leaving behind the only life she'd ever known and journeying with her husband to a new and unseen land. Sarah's heart, faith, and behavior weren't perfect, but even though she may not have understood her future or where she was going, she ultimately trusted the One who knew the outcome.

Genesis 14 includes the first account of a war in Scripture. Abraham and his 318 trained defenders headed out to war to rescue Lot in brutal and violent fighting, similar to what we might see in the movie *Braveheart*. Warfare of this ancient period usually consisted of opposing groups of infantries who fought hand-to-hand with spears, axes, and bows with arrows.[3]

Abraham and his men were small compared to the four kings and their enemies. Abraham took up physical arms and deployed to combat. Sarah likely grappled with fear as Abraham left for war. But she chose not to let her fear have the last word. Sarah likely went to battle too, but with the spiritual armor of prayer. Ephesians 6:18 reminds us that prayer is one of the most potent weapons against our enemy.

It's evident that God heard and answered prayers. God's muscle was on display since he did the impossible deed of bringing victory to Abraham and his 318 men. Abraham had fought against four kings with great military power, but that was nothing compared to the clout and command of God.

Your husband needs you to be his battle buddy and go to war on your knees with spiritual arms. First, we can petition God for our husband to resemble Abraham instead of Lot and be devoted to God rather than power, prestige, or wealth. We can pick up our most potent defense as our husband bravely heads out to war or even deployed territory. Fight your husband's physical, emotional, and spiritual battles using the spiritual weapon of prayer.

Psalm 91 is known as the soldier's psalm. A story from World War I (WWI) indicates that a commander in WWI gave a little card with Psalm 91 on it to his men who were in the 91st Brigade.[4] Facing extreme danger in the trenches with bullets and bombs all around them while they shook with fear, the men of the brigade began to recite the psalm daily. After these men started praying this psalm, they were involved in three of the bloodiest battles in WWI yet suffered no casualties in combat despite other brigades suffering as much as 90 percent.[5]

In Psalm 91, Scripture portrays God as a roaring lion who serves as our refuge, commander, savior, protector, encourager, and mighty fortress.[6] Just like Abraham and Sarah, call upon the Lord to keep your man safe from those who want to cause harm. Using Psalm 91 as a guide, pray the following for your husband when he is serving in harm's way:

- For God to be his fortress
- To be saved from the deadly pestilence
- For God to keep the enemy's weapons far from him
- For your husband to take refuge in the Lord

Pray for your husband's emotional and spiritual well-being by asking God for the following:

- For hope and renewal
- For him to not grow weary
- For him to be content with God as his portion (Lam. 3:21–24)
- For strength and encouragement in his spirit
- For comfort during his deployment
- For courage
- Remember that God is always with him

You might even consider starting a prayer group with those spouses from your unit who have their loved ones away on deployment. Alternatively, if the unit hasn't deployed together, organize a group on your base to welcome anyone with a deployed family member.

REFLECTION

Consider prayer which your husband might need the most now. Pray it over him right now.

What can you do to help ensure you consistently lift these requests for your husband?

PRAYER

Commander of the Army of the Lord, I lift my husband to you today. I ask you to protect him against his physical and spiritual enemies in the shelter of your wing. Give him courage and contentment and help him to be fully devoted to you.

Fortify Yourself

Genesis 14:17–24; Matthew 4:4

Do you ever get "hangry"? I'm generally quite pleasant until I get hungry. *Hanger* is defined as the intense anger and uncomfortable emotions that can come with being hungry. The dictionary added this term in 2018. Abraham clearly knew how to handle his hanger.

Abraham had won the battle, but imagine how weary he must have felt. Like an infantryman, Abraham had come in direct contact with enemy forces and fought physically with their troops. Abraham had probably experienced fear and stumbled to the Valley of Shaveh with his heart pounding, quickened breath, and an overwhelming weary feeling. Just in time, God commissioned a stranger named Melchizedek to fortify him. In Genesis 14:21, the King of Sodom offered Abraham immense earthly wealth, but Abraham resisted this worldly fortification. Instead, God sent just the strength that Abraham needed. Melchizedek provided a meal of bread and wine for the returning visitors.

Bread is used throughout the Scripture to represent the Word of God because it provides true sustenance.[1] Wine usually symbolizes the Spirit or joy, as in Psalm 104:15. Melchizedek was king of Salem, which is related to the Hebrew "shalom," the word for peace.[2] In addition to sustenance, Melchizedek blessed Abraham and reminded him that the Highest God was the possessor of heaven and earth. The bread reminded Abraham that all things belong to God—even deliverance from the enemy. In God's perfect timing, this was the word of encouragement Abraham needed since it was likely that the enemy might attack him in retaliation for his recent defeat of them.[3] Because Abraham had been spiritually fortified beforehand, he was ready when a wicked king offered him earthly riches.[4]

Regular feeding on the Word of God helps us resist temptation. Abraham chose what was eternal instead of what was temporal. Abraham refused the king's riches and took an oath against taking anything from him because he knew anything of value could only come from God. I imagine Abraham let his mistake in Egypt of looking out for himself and acquiring worldly goods teach him where his security resided. Abraham let his mistake teach him humility, and he turned down the world's wealth because he knew riches indeed resided with walking closely with God.[5] Abraham wanted to prosper solely from God's blessings, not a corrupt pagan king.[6]

Abraham didn't react angrily because both bread and a word from God (sent through Melchizedek) had nourished him. Bread was essential to the diet of the ancient world. Due to a lack of preservation methods, people baked bread daily. Early in the Bible, in Deuteronomy 8:3, humans were instructed that "man does not live on bread alone." Moses taught that our dependence on God's Word should be like our reliance on bread. Just like physical nourishment, we should crave God's Word and live in awareness of our need for him and his Word daily.

Jesus had much to say about bread and daily sustenance. Jesus taught the importance of daily feeding of the Word that comes from the mouth of God (Matt. 4:4). When tempted by Satan, Jesus responded by quoting Scripture because he knew it was the most powerful weapon he could use to ward off Satan. Scripture is a powerful armament in our hands and helps us understand God's will and obey it.

Billy Graham summed up the importance of daily feasting on the Word when he said, "If you are ignorant of God's Word, you will always be ignorant of God's will."[7] I'm sure you'd agree that you want to be at the center of God's will. We will know God's will if we consistently feast on his bread.

When my husband was serving in arms, I began to consistently feed on the meat of the Bible by rising earlier than my kids to focus on learning from God's Word. Over the past twenty-five years, the Lord has consistently given me a specific word for a challenge I was facing or direction from the Lord on a decision. It's miraculous to me how, in his sovereignty, God offers me the exact Scripture I need for a troublesome circumstance at precisely the time I need it.

Our physical lives need daily encouragement, but so do our spiritual lives. If you had a day when you went without food, when the next day came, unless you were fasting, you wouldn't continue to resist nourishment if it was available. But, sadly, when we neglect to feed on the Word of God, we often continue that neglect for days, leaving ourselves spiritually malnourished.

Being married to a man serving in the armed forces means you need nourishment in the Word more than you may realize. You, too, have battles to fight for which you need sustenance. You stay on the offensive by consuming God's Word. Even a few minutes while your kids are sleeping or playing can provide what you need to prevent you from being spiritually hangry and help you walk in the Lord's will.

REFLECTION

What are the telltale signs that you're spiritually "hangry" (i.e., when you're neglecting the Word)?

How can you practically spend more time being nourished by the Word this week?

PRAYER

*God Most High, awaken my sense to realize how much I need
the daily sustenance found in your Word. Draw me to your
Word, and by your Holy Spirit, help me thirst for it. I need
a steady diet of your truth, not the junk food and lies this
world offers. Aid me to be satisfied by nothing else but time
with you—and lead my husband to your Word as well!*

Faith over Fear

Genesis 15:1; Philippians 4:6–8

Have you ever gotten in a hot tub or bathtub and watched the water rise as you settled your body into the water? The law of displacement explains the rising water. The law of displacement is a physics principle that tells us that two things cannot fill the same space. In a sense, this law carries over from physics to the mind. We cannot just consciously stop fearful thoughts without replacing them. Max Lucado summed this perfectly: "Feed your fears, and your faith will starve."[1]

Abraham had just enjoyed a mountaintop experience in Genesis 14:14–21. He'd conquered the enemy and God's messenger had fortified him. Although Abraham had been successful in combat with his men, his success didn't appear to be the end of his problems. It was reasonable to assume the kings might retaliate. And so, like many of us after a momentary high, Abraham seems to plunge into the valley of fear and despair by the time we open to Genesis 15:1.[2]

God met Abraham in his despair and delivered a word in a vision. God knew that Abraham needed to build his faith to dispel his fear. In this vision, the Lord reminded Abraham of these words: "I am your shield, your very great reward" (Gen. 15:1 NIV). God was his shield. God affirmed truth to Abraham by retelling him that he'd be his protection no matter the circumstances. God likely knew Abraham's doubtful thoughts and wanted to confirm that his state would be secure despite his resistance of the security the king of Sodom had offered.[3] God would guard Abraham against all danger.

In this vision, God also told Abraham he was his great reward. Abraham need not worry about declining the spoils of war the king offered.[4] Abraham's treasure was God, which was far more than material things.

For Christians, Jesus is our shield and reward. As a shield, he stands between believers and a Holy God and presents himself to receive the penalty for sin on our behalf.[5] This shield protects us from the enemy, Satan. Christ also promises to meet our needs in Philippians 4:19: "And my God will supply all your needs according to his riches in glory in Christ Jesus." A Christian's reward is to receive the right to be coheirs with Christ and a great inheritance with Jesus in eternity.[6]

Philippians 4:6–7 provides the recipe to exchange our anxiety for peace by focusing on faith in God. If you aren't strong in faith, this passage provides the recipe:

> Don't worry about anything, but in everything, through prayer and petition with thanksgiving, present your requests to God. And the peace of God, which surpasses all understanding, will guard your hearts and minds in Christ Jesus.

We build our faith by replacing the enemy's lies with the truth of God and his Word. One of the reasons I need to be in the Word daily is to renew my mind and replace the enemy's negative thoughts and lies with true, honorable, and just thoughts directed by Philippians 4:8:

> Finally brothers and sisters, whatever is true, whatever is honorable, whatever is just, whatever is pure, whatever is lovely, whatever is commendable—if there is any moral excellence and if there is anything praiseworthy—dwell on these things.

I've found that it is just too easy to let fearful thoughts or lies creep into my mind without daily sweeping them out with a fresh dose of the truth of God.

As a military wife, you probably have scary thoughts and questions that your civilian friend has never thought of: Will your husband return safely from combat or deployment? Will your husband remain faithful on deployment? Where will you move next? Will your marriage survive these frequent separations? What will break next in your home when your husband is gone? Can you let go of not being in control of anything in your life? Will your husband get promoted?

Since the law of displacement proves we cannot be full of fear and faith simultaneously, we can replace our fears by focusing on truth. Here is the truth you can rely on: God is sovereign (Jer. 32:17). God is always good (Ps. 119:68). God loves you; perfect love drives out all fear (1 John 4:18). God will never leave you or abandon you (Deut. 31:8). God is your strength (Ps. 73:26). God is your rock, salvation, fortress, and deliverer (Ps. 18:2). Nothing can separate you from God (Rom. 8:38–39). God will strengthen you (Eph. 3:14–16).

Philippians 4:6–7 instructs us to pray instead of worry and to be thankful, which is always possible when we remember God's specific instances of faithfulness in the past. Think of and even write down times God has proven faithful to you. When has he answered prayer? Specifically thank him for these instances of answered prayer. This practice will build your faith that the God who provided before will do so in this situation.

Some days I cannot see past the fog of fear. I need the help of others in Christian community (which is one of the reasons I think it is essential to engage in regular Christian community). On days when I'm weary or discouraged, I'm honest with my sisters in Christ that I need them to help me lift my shield of faith.

Further, on these days, I also remind myself the best way to cast down the lies is to pick up the Truth and read it.

REFLECTION

List five ways God proved faithful to you in the past.

What fears do you need to replace with the truth? Make a list— next to the fear, list the truth to replace it.

PRAYER

My Very Great Reward, thank you for the promise of being my shield and my ultimate gift. Enable me, Father, to stop feeding my fears and instead feed my faith. Alert me to the fears I listen to and help me to displace these fears with memories of your past faithfulness and promises found in your Word.

Waiting

Genesis 15:2–5

Being a military wife provides ample opportunity to learn to wait. Waiting is the standard mode of operation for military families. Waiting on assignments, orders, or for your spouse to call or return from deployment. You may also be waiting for housing and household goods to arrive, or to get a job.

Problem is, most of us don't like to wait. Waiting can cause anger and anxiety and may make us wonder if we matter to God. I've learned that we often wish that God only used microwaves in his kitchen.[1] But God's kitchen has many Crock-Pots because he isn't just cooking the dish; he's maturing us and making us more like Christ. There are important lessons to be learned in God's waiting room.

Waiting can be an opportunity to learn perseverance and more about God's character. Even though we cannot see it, God works in our waiting. You can trust God in the silence. Part of what he is doing is shaping our character and waiting for the right time to accomplish his plan, which is better than our plan. God is using the period to develop the muscles of patience and faith you'll need later. Through the farmer's life, James teaches us in 5:7–13 that patience involves persistent prayer to the Lord; patience is active participation.

In the Bible, God ordained periods of waiting as he was preparing his heroes and heroines for future assignments. Almost every individual listed in the Hebrews 11 Hall of Faith had a time of waiting, preparation, and uncertainty. Hebrews 11 includes both Abraham and Sarah.

Sarah and Abraham found waiting for God's timing regarding their heir's birth extremely difficult. They had already waited many years, and there was still no child. Abraham seems to think God might need assistance orchestrating his plan and that Eleazar, his servant, may be the intended heir. Since Abraham had waited so long for a child and did not yet have an offspring, Abraham thought that his property and inheritance would pass to his servant. From the outside looking in, I wonder if God delayed fulfilling his promise so that Sarah and Abraham would know him better.[2]

Perhaps Abraham was looking too intently at the blessings to come instead of the Blesser himself. Abraham was glaring at his circumstances and lost sight of his God. Our circumstances will always look different when we look at them in light of having looked at God first.[3]

Abraham may have been subtly trying to remind God of his promise when he asked for clarification. Maybe Abraham thought God had forgotten him. Interestingly, God pointed Abraham up instead of down. Abraham had been looking at himself and his situation, which had caused him to doubt. Looking up refocused Abraham on the greatness of God during complex circumstances.

I know in my faith journey that my years of infertility taught me the character of God and gave me time to study and love his Word. I'd never wish infertility on anyone, but my waiting during infertility is the most important factor that shaped who I am today. Yes, it was painful, but it was eventually a tremendous blessing.

Through that journey of waiting, I recognized I needed a Savior and surrendered my life to him. The forced waiting periods caused me to look up and realize that nothing in this world would truly satisfy me, not even a child. God rubbed off some of my rough edges through the waiting. I'd have nothing to write to you right now if I hadn't had that long period of waiting.

While you wait, consider these four practical lessons we can learn from Joseph and David, both of whom waited a long time to be in the position of honor God had promised them:

- **Pray.** David was a man of prayer who penned desperate and raw prayers that make up much of the Psalms. Take this time to talk to God and tell him how you are feeling. He is unfathomably kind and unimaginably strong; he can take it. Ask God to show you what he wants you to learn in this preparation period. While you wait, look in the Bible for his answers.

- **Stop striving.** David could have killed Saul twice and advanced his claim to the throne, but he didn't rush God's will. Friend, you don't have to force something to happen. Even though you may try, you cannot push God's plans. God's timing and methods are always best.

- **Pour out your complaints to God.** David poured out his troubles to God. If you pour out your objections only to other people, at best they may try to understand but lose patience over time, and at worst they might call you a complainer. David was brutally honest with God. He gave God all of his emotions and developed a vibrant prayer life—which might be a reason David was called a "man after [God's] own heart" (1 Sam. 13:14).

- **Do the next thing in front of you.** While you wait, remember that not forcing circumstances doesn't mean you become completely inactive. Joseph is an excellent example of this. Joseph's brothers unjustly sold him into slavery in Egypt. But he glorified God in how he performed the temporary assignments God gave—whether working as an attendant in Potiphar's household or as the head jailer. Joseph's intermediary roles were part of God's divine training ground for him. The place where you find yourself is not a waste.

REFLECTION

What are you waiting for right now?

What two things can you do to prevent yourself from running ahead of the Lord instead of waiting for his answer?

PRAYER

Sovereign Master, I admit I'm not patient and don't wait well. I want to keep my focus on you and not my circumstances. I ask for your help lifting my gaze upon you and trusting in your control of the situation. Assist me in remembering that you are a merciful and compassionate God. Help me to remember that you may be working out other circumstances that I cannot see. I trust you, but help my unbelief.

Day
14

Declared Righteous

Genesis 15:2–6; John 1:12

A *New York Times* editorial asked: "What is wrong with the world today?" The clever but honest writer responded: "Dear sirs, I am. Yours faithfully, G. K. Chesterton."[1] Every one of us can answer in the same manner. Even if you think you are a good person, that is not the test. The Lord declares in his Word that even if we have only broken one of God's laws, we are guilty of breaking them all (James 2:10). More than that, God's Word says we deserve death and eternal separation from God because there is nothing good in us apart from Christ (Rom. 7:18).

When God appeared to Abraham in a vision, Abraham questioned God. Graciously, God condescended to meet Abraham in his lack of faith. Abraham doubted God and his plan to provide him with offspring. Showing his character, God responded with

patience and grace instead of judgment.[2] Abraham responded
with faith in what God had said. It is the same for us; we must
respond confidently to what God says about salvation.

In Genesis 15:1–5, the Lord affirmed, clarified, and ratified
his original promises from a few chapters back (Gen. 12:1–3).
God specifically declared that the offspring of Abraham would
be as numerous as stars in the sky and would be his flesh and
blood. Look at the passage carefully. God declared promises in
verses 1–5. What did Abraham do immediately after this, in verse
6? Nothing. Abraham did nothing. All Abraham did was trust
what God said. Here's how Scripture puts it: "[Abraham] believed
the Lord, and he credited it to him as righteousness." What does
"believed" mean? The Hebrew word translated "believed" in verse
6 means "to support or lean" your whole weight upon.[3] Abraham
leaned wholly on the promise of God and this is what saved him.[4]
Abraham didn't earn this status of righteousness; he was simply
declared righteous because he believed God's assurances.

The Hebrew word translated "credited" (or "counted" in
some translations) means "reckoned or accounted" and is a
bookkeeping term.[5] These terms represent an accurate method
of recordkeeping. So God doesn't just subtract this from our
account; he removes it entirely because he transferred our debt to
the account of Jesus.[6] For Abraham, Jesus had not yet come, but
his promise had been spoken to Sarah and Abraham in Genesis
12:3. In Genesis 12, God promised to bless all families of the
earth through their offspring. John 8:56 tells us that Abraham
rejoiced at the thought of Jesus's coming because his perfect

life and sacrifice provided the substance to the deposit made to Abraham's account.[7]

"Credited it to him as righteousness" also carries a legal meaning. God, in the role of judge, declares that, in his judgment, the person brought before him is not guilty of the accusation against him but instead is in right standing before the law.[8] Abraham's belief placed him in a position of being declared not guilty.

Genesis 15:6 contains one of the essential Christian doctrines because it tells how a person who once displayed nothing but rebellion against God may become right with God.[9] It is not our own works that justify us or declare us righteous; rather, it's the work of another—the work of Christ—that we receive by faith. For Abraham, believing this truth meant looking forward to the coming Savior and banking on his perfect record; for us, it means looking backward to the Savior who has already come, banking on that very same perfect record.

Why could Abraham stand on his own record before God? If you look at Abraham's conduct, he was not righteous. His record had stains all over it. And the same is true for us. I am not righteous; you are not righteous. We need a different record of perfection to stand on in the presence of God—one we could never accomplish ourselves. Thankfully, Christ lived a perfect life; his whole life was acceptable and pleasing to God. Just as Abraham was saved by believing in what God said, we also are saved by believing in what God says about Jesus. We recognize that we cannot earn our salvation. We trust the Word that says we are declared righteous because of our faith in Jesus as God's provision not just for our sins, but also for the righteous life we should have lived all along. For a Christian, God not only declares us not guilty, but he put his Son in our place and paid the penalty on our behalf. Jesus endured the punishment for us so that we may go free. More than that, when we now stand before God, we hold up the life of Christ, and because of our faith in it, we get to be judged by *his* spotless life instead of our own.

Jesus himself told us that Abraham looked forward to the coming Messiah in John 8:56. Abraham would not physically see him, but he saw him with eyes of faith. God had promised that all nations of the earth would be blessed through him. The Messiah who would eventually come from the Jewish people through Jesus was the way that all the nations were blessed.

Christianity separates itself from every other religion because it is the only faith not trying to earn its way to a higher power through good works. Almighty God came down to us in his grace and mercy because he knew we could never earn favor with him. Friend, do you see that? Do you see you don't have to keep striving and failing? You can't measure up, so stop trying! God comes to you and offers you the gift of righteousness because his Son died in your place. The same credit of righteousness made to Abraham's account is available when you choose to rest your life on the Lord and his provision and promises.[10] All it takes to receive this gift is to accept it and believe (John 1:12).

REFLECTION

For what mistakes do you have a hard time accepting God's forgiveness? How does it feel to know you do not have to earn your salvation?

Have you truly received the gift of Jesus? It is more than just an intellectual faith and requires that you genuinely receive him and believe in his name. Receiving Christ means you've put your faith and trust in him alone as your Lord and Savior.

PRAYER

Righteous Judge, thank you for not requiring me to earn your acceptance or be judged by what I've done. How amazing, Lord, that you sent your Son to live a perfect life and die in my place. Allow me to accept your gift of salvation and remind myself regularly what good news it is!

Covenant

Genesis 15:2–21; Jeremiah 31:31–34; Hebrews 8:13; 9:15

Do you have two wedding anniversaries? Many military couples do. The first wedding sometimes occurs at the justice of the peace so that a fiancée can be included on military orders or receive medical benefits. The second ceremony is usually the covenant between man and woman and their God for a lifetime.

Our culture has generally portrayed the marriage covenant to simply be a social contract between two people.[1] In truth, it's much more than that. God intended marriages to showcase the new covenant—the covenant of grace.[2] In the marriage relationship, each person daily realizes their dependence upon God's forgiveness, justification, and promises of future grace because he or she sees their sin so vividly in the day-to-day of marriage.[3]

Further, the marriage covenant represents the bond between Christ and the church. Somewhere along the way, we've heard our culture tell us that individualism is more important than a promise. Society tells us we can get permission to revoke our commitment if we are disappointed in our marriage. We forget it is a solemn promise before God to honor, esteem, and care for our mate until death do us part.

To better understand the marriage covenant, it is crucial to understand the covenant between God, Abraham, and Sarah. In ancient culture, covenants were agreements between enemies or battling groups entered into to join against a common enemy.[4] Under the new covenant, those who believe in Christ can enjoy the benefits of a relationship with God. Abraham's covenant ceremony guaranteed God's promise to Abraham and Sarah and provided a significant memory that could be clung to when faith wavered.

God commanded Abraham to gather five particular animals of specified ages. Due to the specificity, Abraham did not wonder what God was asking him to do—he knew God was asking him to gather the animals that were used in covenant ceremonies common in Abraham's time.[5] In this religious ritual, animals were cut in half with the two pieces laid opposite each other, and then both parties would pass between the divided carcasses and meet in the middle to signify the intensity and importance of their vow. Abraham probably gathered the animals with a bit of nervousness and trepidation, wondering what type of covenant he and God would create. The ceremony dramatized a self-imposed curse if either of the parties broke their pledge; the parties effectively stated, "I will die like these animals if I don't live up to my obligations of the covenant."[6]

Notice that apart from setting up the animals, Abraham wasn't allowed to participate in the ceremony when it came time to pass through the carcasses.[7] God caused him to fall asleep. God traveled the bloody path alone because he was unilaterally making the covenant.[8] In other words, God was promising something to this effect: "If I don't keep my end of the covenant, may what happened to these animals happen to me. And, on top of that, since I'm taking your place in the ceremony and not allowing you to pass through, I will journey fully to the other side, covering the path you should have walked. With that, I'm also promising that if *you* don't keep *your* end of the covenant—even if you fail—may what happened to these animals still happen to me. Should you fail on your end, I will take the hit for it. I'm putting the weight of this covenant entirely on my own shoulders."

God signified his presence with two symbols—a smoking pot and a flaming torch.[9] Although the Scripture doesn't explain the meaning, we can look to ancient culture and other Scriptures for interpretation. In ancient history, a burning pot was well-known to purify metals. A metal worker heated the furnace until the impure part separated from the metal and rose to the top; he then skimmed it off.[10] God also appeared to the Israelites by night in a smoking fire. The second symbol was the blazing torch, which symbolized God's presence. God is called "light" in John 1:5 and appeared as light when he led the Israelites through the desert.

Jesus also spoke to Paul on the road to Damascus and appeared as light. In short, the pot and torch communicate God's purifying presence was truly *there* at this covenant scene. Abraham was not making a covenant with some other ordinary man or a pagan god. Make no mistake: he was entering into covenant with Yahweh, the one true God of the heavens and the earth.

As the smoking pot and flaming torch passed through the bloody animal pieces, let's recall what God was essentially saying: "Abraham, I'll walk through the bloody path on your behalf because I know you are going to mess it up."[11] Since Abraham would not be able to keep the agreement, God was the one who would pay the price. Even before God made the covenant, he knew he'd pay the price of dying just like the animals he passed through.

God did pay the price of the covenant when he provided the sacrifice of his Son. God himself, in the person of Jesus, was the one who paid the price for man's side of the broken covenant.

God was also teaching Sarah and Abraham an essential aspect of his character—he is compassionate and gracious.[12] He would care for them even when they messed up and disobeyed. Even though God did care for them, Abraham and Sarah did have to face some consequences.

Why spend time on understanding this covenant? Because this covenant is so relevant today. If you have placed your faith in Jesus, you are a party to the new covenant (Heb. 9:15). When we put our faith in Christ, similar to how he did with Abraham, God says, "I know you are going to make a mistake; but when you make a mistake, I'll pay the price. My Son will pay the price by dying in your place."[13] Just as God made a covenant with Sarah and Abraham and kept it through history, he has made a covenant with all Christians that will last through eternity.[14]

With a better understanding of the seriousness of a covenant in general, it is crucial to evaluate the seriousness with which we view the specific covenant of marriage. Marriage to a military man will not be easy. Neither is it easy for God to selflessly keep his covenant with believers. God's standard for keeping a covenant isn't convenience or fulfillment. God designed marriage to be a unique display of his covenant grace because the husband and wife are bound by covenant into the nearest possible relationship for a lifetime.[15] Treasuring your marriage covenant will test your capacity and strength at various points, but it is ultimately a response to the grace and love that God has shown you.

REFLECTION

Grace is undeserved favor. How do you see God's grace in the covenant ceremony he executed with Abraham?

As stated earlier, most people in today's time view marriage as a contract or social arrangement and forget it is a solemn and binding agreement between man, wife, and God. Why do you think this is the case?

PRAYER

Covenant Maker, thank you so much for being willing to make a covenant with Abraham you knew he couldn't keep. Thank you for remaining faithful and performing your part. I want to live out my gratitude that your Son died in my place because you knew I'd disobey. Help me live this out in how I love and respect my husband. I've not taken the marriage covenant as seriously as I should. Help me to remain committed.

Flourishing vs. Fierce

Genesis 2:18; 16:1–6; Ephesians 5:22–23, 33

Yet again, the military moved us across the country. While unpacking and setting up home, my husband took leave to ease our transition into the new place. Since I was homeschooling then, I had the challenge of keeping my kids learning while also unpacking boxes. I'm used to unloading dishes while delivering spelling tests, but not unpacking boxes while teaching algebra. Since my husband was home, he graciously thought he could assist with algebra and got involved in the day's lesson. I'm embarrassed to say that I did not share my home turf with my husband. I was allowing him to lead in certain areas while withholding his input from others. We were arguing more frequently than normal due to my opposition to him invading my space.

One evening, my husband gently spoke the truth to me: "I have always been a natural leader in my life. I successfully led my high school senior class; I led my ROTC cadet core as commander in college; and I even led a squadron of three hundred enlisted and officers, but I can't lead you." Ouch! But it was profoundly true. I was the problem.

You may think a two-headed serpent is the stuff of mythology, but did you know a snake with two heads exists in California? A version of the king snake is born with two heads due to genetic mutations. Born in the wild, these snakes die right away. With two heads usually moving in opposite directions, the snake struggles to progress movement. Its limited mobility makes it much more susceptible to predators.[1] The snake's organs are overworked and the body endures excessive stress; ultimately, this snake destroys itself.[2] The only way for a snake like this to survive is to live in captivity.

Like a two-headed snake, we see Sarah challenging Abraham's leadership in their family in the account of Hagar. God had promised Abraham that he would have a son through whom God would bless all nations of the world. Eleven years had passed since God had initially made that promise, but he had recently confirmed it in a ceremony. In his leadership, Abraham shared God's promise with Sarah. Yet, Sarah grew impatient and lost trust in Abraham and, ultimately, in God. She rose against Abraham's leadership and eventually convinced him to follow her plan of making a child through her maidservant, Hagar. Consequences ensued for them all. Sarah's choice to rise as a competing head to Abraham was an awful idea and prevented her from thriving in her relationship with God and with Abraham. As military wives, we can learn from Sarah's example and resist opposing our husband's leadership in a manner that crushes him. For each family to flourish and move in a united direction, we can willingly submit to our husband's leadership as an act of obedience to the Lord.

I imagine you are a lot like me; you're a military spouse, which means you are a strong woman with her own opinions—a woman who often has to independently steer the ship of your home and life. Your strong personality helps you navigate the seasons of single parenting and conquer all the challenges that military life expects of you. However, this strong and independent personality, when used in sinful ways instead of helpful ways, can crush your husband and damage your marriage. I hope you can learn from my and Sarah's mistakes how to resist stifling your husband with an aggressive spirit and, instead, be a mate who encourages her man and helps him flourish.

Although the Lord equally values the wife, the Lord sets the husband as the head just as Christ is the head of the church (Eph. 5:22–23). So God calls a wife to give detailed, thoughtful, and glad submission to her husband's leadership.[3] This involvement means the wife doesn't sin by aggressively dominating her husband and undermining his authority.[4] Keep in mind: this does not mean she acts in passive ways, never speaks up, or refuses to participate in decision-making! She is balanced between the two because she ultimately submits herself to the Lord and trusts that even if she disagrees with her husband's decision, the wife trusts God. Of course, a wife should not submit to a husband who is abusing her physically or emotionally or abusing his authority over her.

God calls the wife to respect her husband while he calls the husband to sacrificially love his wife (Eph. 5:33). When God made Eve, he called her a "helper" for Adam. As explained on Day 4, the helper role is not a subservient or lower role, but is a role of great importance. If our words, tone, or behavior are crushing to our man, we likely aren't respecting him and are not giving him life. A man needs respect like a fish needs water. So considering whether a wife is harsh or inspiring her man to flourish impacts how she communicates respect to her husband. Gentleness in speech would effectively communicate respect to your husband. Follow the example of Jesus who deals gently with those who are going astray (Heb. 5:2).

Both husband and wife are to treat and speak to one another with kindness. True character of any disciple of Jesus includes speech seasoned with grace that builds one another up (Eph. 4:29). Jesus commanded his followers to love their neighbor as their self (Mark 12:31). Certainly, our spouse is our neighbor in closest proximity. Encouraging words will go a long way as you cheer for your man and help him rise to be a husband who will love you sacrificially.

This book is written to you as the wife, but I want you to know that a husband is called to use an encouraging and gentle tone with his wife as well. First Peter 3:7 calls a husband to show honor to his wife, while Colossians 3:19 instructs him against being harsh with his wife. The role of headship does not give a husband free rein to speak or act disparagingly to his wife.

To assess whether you are adding flourishing encouragement or fierce opposition, consider if you see some of these symptoms in your marriage. Your husband may respond to your aggressive manner by shutting down, responding in harsh anger, or passively retreating to his own silent world.[5] A combative woman will also be loud, pushy, obnoxious, arrogant, often ranting and demanding her way.[6] Wives have an enormous power of influence over their husbands; they can use it to either inspire their man or destroy him.[7] What will you do?

REFLECTION

Which description do you most identify with, fierce or flourishing? Are there any symptoms in your husband's behavior that indicate you might be fierce?

How can you gracefully share your views but ultimately allow your husband to lead the family?

PRAYER

Good Shepherd, thank you for not being fierce in your rule over me. I admit I see symptoms of either combativeness or passivity in how I interact with my husband. Help me be more gracious to my husband and resist vitriolic opposition. Aid me in enhancing my husband's authority by thoughtfully contributing without undermining it. I thank you, Lord, that I have the Holy Spirit to assist me in gently supporting my husband.

The God Who Sees

Genesis 16:7–16; 21:15–21

I slumped on the bathroom floor as tears trickled down my face and then I burst into tears. I was tired of being strong. With two kids under three and my husband gone again, I felt like giving up. We were living in Korea; I missed my family and husband and longed for a normal life. It had been one of those days when nothing went well. It never fails that when your husband leaves on temporary duty (TDY) or deployment, that something breaks, or someone gets sick. It's an unwritten rule in military life. We jokingly blame our friend, "Murphy." This time it wasn't anything significant, it was the dehumidifier. In Korea, the dehumidifier is a small convenience that makes the climate more bearable. It was hot and muggy, and the kids were just missing their dad, which usually made them more challenging to handle. In their toddler and preschool years, kids just can't cope with Daddy being gone—especially when they don't have an effective mechanism to communicate their frustration. So they throw tantrums and behave more defiantly than usual. I was weary. I can guess you've been there too, friend.

I'm not going to lie; military-wife life can sometimes be terribly challenging. The Father sees those who suffer, especially women. We see this in the account of Hagar. Just like he saw Hagar when she was sitting by the spring of water in the wilderness, he sees you, military wife. He cares. You are his beloved daughter.

After Sarah's bad idea to have Hagar conceive a child with Abraham in Genesis 16, conflict arose between Sarah and Hagar. Sarah mistreated Hagar, and Hagar fled into the wilderness where an "angel of the LORD" found her near a spring. This appearance of the "angel of the LORD" to Hagar is the first time Scripture mentions this phrase. Although somewhat debated, most theologians believe this was not just an angel but a pre-incarnate manifestation of Jesus.[1] Other thinkers believe that this was a self-manifestation of God the Father.[2] Either of these are reasonable since the angel speaks in first person as if he is God, is equated with God, and can manifest himself in many ways.[3]

Beyond the garden of Eden, this is one of the first mentions of God appearing to a person. Do you recognize the significance here—that the first person God appeared to in this form was a *woman* and not just a woman, but a lowly servant? Not only was she a servant, but she was oppressed and distressed. Hagar had no stature in the world's terms, yet was an explicit object of God's love and provision. Hagar felt abandoned and lonely too. God sees you where you are and cares for you as you are.[4] God is especially attentive to the cry of the distressed.[5] Do you see the Father's love and esteem for you, his daughter?

When this manifestation of God appears to Hagar, he responds with patience and gentle grace by first asking her questions.[6] Then, God established a promise of great blessing using similar language to the benefit applied to Isaac and Israel in Genesis 22:17.[7] Here's his blessing: "I will greatly multiply your offspring, and they will be too many to count" (Gen 16:10). To such unexpected grace and blessing, Hagar responded to God by naming him *El-Roi*, which means "the God who sees me." God not only saw her, but he also sought her out. We learn from this encounter that God is more interested in us than we can ever be interested in him.[8] God never fails to see what is going on; he is vitally interested in everything that touches one of his creatures.[9]

The angel of the Lord instructed Hagar to return to Sarah. He wanted her to adjust her attitude, return, and start over. We, too, have the same opportunity to return to the point where we went wrong and start over. Praise God, his mercies are new every morning, and it's always morning somewhere.

Hagar named her son Ishmael, which means "God hears" and was the name the angel of the Lord instructed her to use for her son. Since Abraham allowed his son to be named Ishmael, it is likely that Abraham allowed Hagar to relay her encounter with God after she had returned from the meeting with God at the spring. Through this name, God was saying that he hears the cry of the afflicted.[10]

God sees you. He hears your cries. He knows your needs. He cares. Through Hagar, we've learned that God provides loving guidance and careful protection for his children.[11] God wants to be actively involved in your affairs. He will come if you call upon him in prayer.

REFLECTION

What circumstances of military life cause you to feel the most afflicted?

How can you reach out to God to ask him to become more involved in your day-to-day struggles as a military wife? How might you remind yourself that God sees and cares for you during those times?

PRAYER

El Roi, thank you that even though I sometimes feel alone as a military wife, you are with me. Thank you that you chose to reveal yourself to Hagar, and you decided to show yourself to me now. Help me to adjust my attitude and start over right now with a renewed hope for recognizing the opportunity you've blessed me with as a military wife. I realize I cannot make this journey alone, and I need you, Lord.

Hard Roads

Genesis 17:1–8; Romans 4:19–21

Like Sarah, I also had to walk the lonely road of infertility. During the height of our inability to conceive, the military stationed us at a training base. Though our culture didn't consider infertility as socially taboo as it was for Sarah, it was still a hard and unwelcome road. In our training unit, baby showers were a monthly activity. I was happy celebrating our friends' good news, but the showers made my empty womb ache.

Eventually, God led us to adoption, and we joyfully welcomed home an eight-month-old baby boy from overseas. Like Sarah, my hard road of infertility led to spiritual maturity. I'd learned to trust a God whose plans and purposes I didn't quite understand. I had learned to look not to my situations but to my God, who was above them. I eventually knew that if God had closed my womb, it was because he had a much greater plan for our family. God had chosen us to welcome a child into our home whose home country conditions meant it would be terribly unlikely for him to ever hear about a saving Lord. God closed my womb to open our eyes to a greater mission.

Thirteen years had passed between the birth of Ishmael and Genesis 17, so it was now *twenty-four years* from the original promise. God appeared to Abraham and identified himself as "God Almighty." This instance is the first time God identifies himself as such. This name means the strong one, the all-sufficient one, or the all-powerful one.

Since Abraham was ninety-nine and Sarah was eighty-nine, no one but an all-powerful God could meet their needs.[1] God may have been telling Abraham that God's purposes cannot be thwarted by anything, including aging bodies.[2] God had the sufficiency to fulfill his promises to cause an aged man and a woman beyond childbearing years to conceive a child.[3]

God instructed Abraham to "walk before me" (Gen. 17:1 ESV). God may have asked this of Abraham because it communicated that the Almighty God would protect him, be just behind him, and take care of him and his seed.[4] God's command for Abraham to walk before him and be blameless wasn't a condition of the covenant but was a response to the covenant already made.[5]

Abraham and Sarah's faith walk had been long, but it seemed to have built some spiritual maturity as they waited on God fulfilling the promise. "Walking with God" also speaks to spiritual maturity. God spoke of walking with other Old Testament characters—Moses (Exod. 33:11), Enoch (Gen. 5:22–24), and Noah (Gen. 6:9).[6] God had fellowship, friendship, and harmony with these other characters. God wanted Abraham to continue to walk with him, but he was reminding him that he'd give him the grace to continue to do so.[7] Abraham was so overwhelmed with the grace of God shown to him that he fell on his face and worshipped as he saw the grace of God despite his previous unbelief.[8]

God articulated how powerful he was by renaming Abraham the father of multitudes and confirming his covenant. God would create the line of the Messiah through Abraham and Sarah, who were barren. Because God had all power, he fulfilled his promise to Sarah and Abraham.

Romans 4:19–21 tells us that Abraham faced the fact that his body was good as dead and Sarah's womb was dead, yet did not waiver in unbelief regarding the promise. Abraham now knew that God had the power to do what he had promised. God always fulfills what he has promised. Since God is the Creator, he can affect all things. There is nothing too hard for the Lord (Jer. 32:17).

God's all-sufficiency can be trusted even though your circumstances don't look encouraging. When the details of your life don't align with your timing or directions, learn more about the Lord and grow closer to him. Just like Sarah and I grew spiritually during our waiting time, you, too, can move toward the Lord during your pause. Unlike a hospital waiting room, God's waiting room is always a good place to be because he longs to meet with you and welcome you into intimacy with him.

Recognize that Abraham's God is our God.[9] There is nothing that is outside of God's almighty power in your life. Just like God made Sarah's dead womb alive, God can work miraculously in your life.

Sometimes we miss miracles because they don't look like what we think they should. We get an idea of what we believe the circumstances should be and miss God's better plan for us. As a military wife, your circumstances can seem outside of the control of the Almighty God. God is powerful enough to control your challenge. God wants you to depend upon him and walk your hard road alongside him. Some hard roads you might be facing include:

- Your next assignment
- Your spouse's deployment
- Living overseas
- Your failing marriage
- Your spouse's combat trauma (including PTSD and other invisible wounds of war)
- Your loneliness
- Your ability to balance single parenting with your spouse deployed or TDY
- Infertility

(Please note there are resources for those struggling with combat trauma. Military REBOOT offers trauma healing courses that specifically address combat trauma, spiritual wounds of war, and include the spouse in the healing course. I've personally witnessed remarkable transformation through this course.)

REFLECTION

Name two things you struggle to believe God is powerful enough to control.

What is one way in which you can grow spiritually while you wait for God to ease your hard road?

PRAYER

God Almighty, enable me to remember today that you are my helper. No matter what hard road you have ordained for me, you will be right beside me during the journey. Help me remember that you are powerful enough to control every detail of my circumstances and trust that when you say, "No!" it is because you have a greater plan. Help me walk before you faithfully.

Building a Legacy

Genesis 17:9–27

After attending countless military promotion and retirement ceremonies, I've learned it is common to have several generations of family members who wore the uniform and served their country. Moms, dads, and grandfathers beam with the pride they feel at the legacy of service to the country their relative is continuing. It's common to come across a family that views the military as their family business. If you aren't serving in uniform, that doesn't mean you cannot leave a legacy. Your legacy may be even more important than one of military service. A legacy is something of value passed down or received from one who came before us. God desires both you and your husband to pass along a legacy of faith that will impact the world, now and even after you are gone.

The topic of circumcision might make you squirm, but it is a graphic picture of the importance of passing our faith to the next generation. Believe it or not, circumcision points to the gospel.

When God reaffirmed the covenant with Abraham again in chapter 17, he spoke seven "I will" statements in which he created and established the terms.[1] God initiated and carried out the terms of the agreement, which was a product of his grace. Then, God changed Abraham's name as if to say, "This covenant ties me to you forever; there is no turning back."

Circumcision, or the cutting away of the flesh, was symbolic of renouncing all human effort.[2] In the Bible, "flesh" often refers to our sinful state as humans.[3] The flesh was cut away to show that human activity is without effect on salvation and also that God's people must be separated (or set apart) from the world. God wanted Abraham to have this permanent mark to remind himself of his identification with and commitment to God. This mark could not be severed and stood for something that was based solely upon what God did, not man.

Circumcision wasn't a condition of God's blessings upon Abraham. His justification was effected through faith, just like faith in Jesus allows a believer to be accepted.[4] The sign of circumcision was a physical reminder of the righteousness that God had given Abraham due to his belief in God's promise. The outward circumcision was to reflect the "circumcision" of the heart that was unseen but very real.[5]

The mark of the covenant was something that all future believers in the one true God, Yahweh, would take with them wherever they went.[6] In their ancient culture, monotheism (the belief in one god) was an odd practice and was a definitive mark of a Jewish person who believed in God.[7] In their culture, this mark defined who you were because it was so different, and no one else had it.[8] Then, Jewish families kept this practice in a step of obedience. So they would have circumcised all their male babies on the eighth day to physically mark them as followers of the God of Israel.

Since the Jewish family held a sacred ceremony on the eighth day, the practice was explained to all family members, and the little Jewish boys knew why they looked different. It was because they worshipped and served the one true God, who was the God of grace.

God wants us to pass on the legacy of faith. After Jesus's incarnation, death, and resurrection, circumcision is no longer required (1 Cor. 7:18–19). So we pass down our legacy in other ways that operate as gospel reminders of our participation in the New Covenant community—baptism and the Lord's Supper. Just as other covenants come with signs, the "signs" of baptism and Communion are visual reminders of deep spiritual truths. As new believers go down into the water, they signify that they have died with Christ. As they are raised out of the water, they signify their great future—that they will pass through the waters of death and rise to new life, just like Christ did in his resurrection. Through the Lord's Supper, believers remember the body and blood of Christ, shed for them on the cross. By bringing our children or others to regular church gatherings, we give them the opportunity to see visual symbols of what we believe in the gospel of grace, which we haven't earned.

Since your husband will likely be deployed, away on TDY orders, or working long hours, you'll get to put a lot of muscle and time into passing along a legacy of faith to your offspring. Even if you don't have children, you can pass along a legacy of faith to those in your sphere of influence in all the military installations where you will live or visit. If you have kids, consider discussing this with your husband and get his input on passing along a legacy of faith to your children. Along with regularly bringing these loved ones into a church gathering where they can witness the signs of the New Covenant, here are five other ideas for passing down your faith:

- **Faith is caught, not taught.** Let your kids see you regularly and intentionally pursuing your relationship with God.
- **Model praying without ceasing.** What a great example to set for your family that you pray about even the little things throughout your day.
- **Weave the gospel into everyday conversations with your kids.** When your kids disobey, correct and remind them what a blessing it is that we don't have to be perfect because Jesus took the penalty on our behalf. Incorporate the goodness of God into regular conversations.

- **You aren't a perfect mom; don't pretend to be.** One of the most beautiful ways to point your kids to the gospel is to admit when you sin, ask for their forgiveness, and pray to God together.
- **Read the Bible together.** It doesn't have to be sophisticated. When my kids were little, we would act out a simple Bible story, complete with whatever props we had in the dress-up box.

REFLECTION

What is one way you can intentionally invest in leaving a legacy of faith at the base where you are stationed right now?

Which of the above suggestions for leaving a legacy will you try to implement this week?

PRAYER

My Redeemer, help me to impart the importance of faith in you to those in my sphere of influence. I want to be set apart as one who worships the one true God and influences others to worship you. Help me keep my heart circumcised for you, which will allow me to cling to the reality of the gospel of grace and share that with others.

Day 20

Single Parenting

Genesis 16:7–15; 21:1–21; Matthew 11:28; James 1:5

My active-duty friend had a husband stationed on the other side of the country. Toward the end of her pregnancy, she called me early one morning and asked if I could come to her aid at the hospital. She was in labor while her husband was still en route, but likely wouldn't arrive before the baby. Joyfully, I got to coach her as she brought another precious human into the world.

Another friend of mine eagerly waited for the arrival of her Army husband who had been deployed for over nine months. As her husband exited the secured area of the airport, he ran to her and gave her a sincere hug and kiss and then asked to see his first child who was sitting in the car seat beside the mom and hadn't yet had the chance to meet her daddy. Two years later, this dear friend introduced her husband to their second child in much the same manner in the baggage claim area of the airport. You often must parent your children alone while the military sends your spouse elsewhere.

We've already looked at the account of Hagar sent off into the desert and how God sees us when we are in anguish as military wives. Hagar also had to endure a season of single parenting after Sarah had her own baby, Isaac. Sarah sent Hagar and Ishmael away to minimize conflict. This treatment was undoubtedly unfair to Hagar, but God allowed it because Isaac was the son of promise, and therefore all the firstborn rights as Abraham's heir needed to go to him.

Hagar found herself in the desert and ran out of provisions. In her desolate tears, she thought her son would die. God heard the cries and cared for them. God spoke and reassured Hagar of his care and promised to make Ishmael a great nation.[1] God opened Hagar's eyes to the nearby water well and provided for her. God also sees us during our seasons of single parenting.

As a single parent, even temporarily, you have probably felt you cannot cope. You are worn out and frustrated with all the demands of parenting and running the household alone. You may always feel tired. I get it! You long for peace, quiet, and a break from the hectic pace. You may even feel weary and burdened.

Whatever stage of single parenting you are in, just like God initially saw Hagar by the spring, he sees you. Just as he heard Hagar and her son's cries and aided them, he will come to you. God is with you even though you may feel alone. He is tenderhearted and cares for you. God has not forgotten you. God promises to give rest to those who are weary if they come to him (Matt. 11:28).

Some tips for navigating the temporary single-parenting gig include seeking God for wisdom, maintaining an appropriate schedule balance, practicing self-care, continuing routine, and making your husband's presence known to your kids.

The challenges of single parenting may cause you to feel like you don't know what to do. God is all-knowing. His Word can guide many parenting struggles. James 1:5 tells us if we lack wisdom, we are to ask God, who gives generously to all. Even if your parenting answer isn't found directly in Scripture, it can provide you the peace to keep your patience and the mental clarity to discern what to do. Protect your time in the Word; it is a life preserver to a drowning soul. Cling to God when you don't have your spouse to cling to physically.

Maintaining a balanced schedule is essential. Make a list of each activity of you and your kids. Evaluate whether each activity ministers to you or others. Quickly eliminate activities that don't minister to either. Carefully consider other activities that only meet one category. Recognize you are in a hard season and might not be able to handle as many activities as you might when your spouse is home. It's okay to say no in order to add more peace and balance to your life! You'll likely find your stress level will decrease as you lower your commitments.

While some may define self-care as self-indulgence and boundless pampering, practicing self-care, in my definition, is simply being mindful of your limits and needs. It is not selfish to care for yourself, so you are healthy enough to care for little humans. Jesus withdrew for times of self-care when he prayed, worshipped, and submitted to the will of God. So we must care for our bodies to care for humans. Take time to exercise, eat well, and sleep to care for your mental and spiritual well-being. Self-care might include regular counseling with a Christian counselor or being involved in a Bible study that will enrich you spiritually. With a deployed spouse, put the kids to bed early or allow them to watch some limited media while you get mental or physical rest. With a deployed spouse, cereal or macaroni and cheese are sufficient for dinner!

Routine helps everyone maintain a cool head when the kids are little and the husband is away. As much as possible, continue the kids' schedule.

Make your husband's presence known to your kids as much as possible. I suggest posting pictures of your husband around your house, the crib, or the bathroom mirror. Give your kids shirts or blankets with your husbands' scent. Use technology as much as possible to allow your kids to interact with their dad.

Your faith in God is your most potent and powerful weapon—prioritize him above all else.

REFLECTION

Since God tells us to seek him for wisdom, how can you specifically seek the Lord for parenting wisdom today?

How can you adjust your schedule for more balance or adequate self-care?

PRAYER

Father of Compassion, thank you that I know you see me and my struggle with handling parenting by myself. Help me adjust my expectations of myself and my children to adequately account for our missing dad. Enable me to remember that you are my ultimate provider and to look to your guidance and wisdom with parenting my kids. Allow me to see appropriate boundaries and balance with our schedule.

Hospitality

Genesis 18:1–8; 1 Peter 4:9

I went on a mission trip aimed at spiritual conversations with Middle Easterners. Middle Easterners put a cultural premium on hospitality.[1] The hospitality these strangers showed me was admirable and transformed my view of hospitality. Nervously, I approached a group of picnicking ladies. Within two minutes, they insisted I share their meal. They heaped large portions onto my plate and gave me a water bottle. This hospitality has been part of Middle Eastern culture since the time of Sarah.

In Genesis 18, when the three visitors visited Abraham and Sarah, Sarah quickly baked bread with flour. Then, she and Abraham hurried to serve their visitors a calf and milk. Sarah and Abraham lived in a tent, so I doubt it was picture-perfect, but they extended hospitality to their visitors. Sarah and Abraham readily pursued hospitality and fellowship as they opened their humble tent.

In a study by Dr. Holt-Lunstad, loneliness was as lethal as smoking fifteen cigarettes daily.[2] As a military wife, you possess valid reasons to be lonely. Your forced mobility disrupts friendships and separates your family. But you can make a change to improve your mental and physical well-being. You may be tired of moving and initiating companionship, which results in closing yourself off. Even as you feel lonely, countless others feel that way too. The solution is community with God and others.

Did you know our technological devices inhibit our connection with others and make us lonely?[3] God created us to have a relationship with him and with others. The entire Bible focuses on our need for communion with God and others.

I challenge you to invite others to your home for community. Make the first move toward genuine face-to-face friendship with hospitality. Inviting others over doesn't have to be social media–worthy. Social media doesn't give us a biblical view of the command to exercise hospitality.

We get the wrong view of hospitality when we think our house needs to be perfect. I know this phenomenon is not limited because someone created a new term in the dictionary explaining what we do when we prepare for company. Although you may not know this specific term, I suspect you've done it. You have guests coming to your home in thirty minutes and you are rushing around mad trying to pick up all the mess and clean the house so that it looks less lived-in. You may even bark orders at your husband and kids in an angry tone to get them to hop to it. *Scurryfunge* is the term that describes the hurried rush of cleaning before visitors arrive. I used to do that, truth be told, but I soon learned I had to adjust my view of hospitality because I needed to obey the Scripture that called me to offer hospitality without complaining (1 Pet. 4:9).

We had just moved to a new base; I was lonely and wanted community. I opened my home weekly for Bible study and adjusted my view of what our home needed to be to welcome others. I surrendered the idea of a spotless house but decided to welcome people into my home with its imperfections. Inviting others with scattered toys, clutter on the counter, and even some dirty dishes is acceptable. I served folks leftovers for dinner because that was what we had available. Generally, I just stir up a pitcher of lemonade and brew some coffee. Hospitality opens your life up for God's glory. It's moving from being self-focused to thinking about those around you. "Hospitality is about connection, not perfection."[4] Or, as I like to say, *people matter more than presentation.*

Two reasons for hospitality are to extend your connection and minister to others, which is obeying God's command. Just as you are lonely, others also feel alone. Engage in hospitality to reach others and offer hope. Henry Nouwen provides this perspective: "Hospitality is not to change people but to offer them space where change can take place."[5] By inviting others over, you might get the opportunity to point them to your source of hope.

The gospel is the greatest news we've ever heard! Jesus died to take the penalty for our sins for all who believe in him.

Initiating relationships with others who are lonely can open doors for you to discuss faith and what Jesus has done for you. Everyone in your sphere deserves to hear such freeing information! Rosaria Butterfield says, "Those who live out radically ordinary hospitality see their homes not as theirs at all but as God's gift to use for the furtherance of his kingdom. They open doors; they seek out the underprivileged."[6]

You can be open to extending hospitality to others, initiating relationships, and vulnerably taking risks to get to know others. It is easy to live lonely as a military wife, but then you are missing out on so much great community and all the people you could form relationships with whom you can positively impact and can impact you. The risk is worth it; get out of your comfort zone and get blessed!

REFLECTION

Are your expectations too high when inviting people over? How can you adjust your expectations?

How can you extend hospitality to another military wife or family this week?

PRAYER

God of Strangers, I want to obey your command to extend hospitality to others to minister to them and create a pathway for gospel conversations. Guide me to lower my expectations for my home to open my heart to others. Help me to develop healthy friendships. Give me eyes to see those around me who are lonely and to whom I can minister by opening my home.

Unbelief

Genesis 18:9–21; Jeremiah 32:27

As I said in Day 18, I struggled with infertility, which pointed me to my need for Christ and caused me to explore and surrender to the gospel. As a new believer, I didn't know nothing was impossible for the Lord (which Sarah discerned in Genesis 18). The doctors had convinced me that fertility drugs were how I'd be able to conceive. Through Jeremiah 32:27 and Genesis 16–18, God revealed that I had not given God complete control of my life since I was still trusting in medication to conceive. I was struggling with unbelief. (None of that is to say that medication is wrong; but for me and my story, I realized I had promoted medication to "first place" in my struggle instead of God.) I agreed with God that I lacked faith in his sovereignty over my body's ability to conceive and asked his help to relinquish control.

After settling into the joy of being a mother with our first child, adopted from Russia, I fully yielded to God's plan for our family. I'd moved from thinking adoption was second best to realizing it was a privilege to welcome an orphaned child. My husband and I began a second adoption process with the agency that orchestrated our first adoption. Previously, I had falsely thought I had control over my body with medical intervention. I finally gave up control and moved from unbelief to belief in God's ability to open my womb. I was content to trust God even if he chose to keep me barren.

The following month, God showed us he was the only person controlling anything. I was able to conceive a child in a manner only made possible by God! I finally became content whether or not he decided to keep me barren. And then God surprised me with a blessing. He doesn't always do the exact same thing in every person's story, but for me, he amazed me with this unexpected twist in my fertility journey.

We learn in Genesis 17:17 that Abraham laughed at the prospect of bearing a son, and then Sarah laughed in 18:12 when she overheard that she'd have a son. Although it might seem like Abraham and Sarah responded similarly, God's reaction indicates a different heart motivation in their laughter. Abraham's chuckle didn't reveal unbelief but more that he was amused at the thought of him being a father at the age of one hundred.[1] Romans 4:19–22 gives us evidence that Abraham's laughter didn't indicate a lack of faith because it says God had convinced Abraham that he had the power to fulfill his promises.

In contrast, Sarah was fearful and faithless. Sarah's laughter was an expression of utter unbelief, as the response of the Lord indicates.[2] Sarah's laughter was more of scorn and showed contempt.[3] Sarah's denial of her laughter reveals that she thought it was impossible for her to bear a child since she passed her childbearing years and didn't have a functioning womb. Her laughter indicated her lack of trust in God.[4] God confronted Sarah's laughter because he wanted her to be transparent about her fears.[5] God wanted Sarah's complete confidence.

Trying to control the details of life can make you weary. Control is the enemy of rest. When you think you've lost control, a natural tendency is to hold tighter to your facade of control. You grip harder or strive more but get nowhere. Jesus wants you to come to him and release control into his loving arms. Let go of your firm grip on control—after all, the only way to receive what God is holding out to you is to open up your hands.

Genesis 18:11 made it clear that there was no natural possibility for Sarah to have a son, but there is nothing too hard for the Lord. God had promised Sarah and Abraham a son. What God promises, he can perform. God was able to cause the impossible with Sarah's aging body. God also wants to work the impossible through us if we allow him to do so.[6] Since God is the Creator of all, he can do anything. God still does miracles and certainly did with Sarah. God used Sarah as a human instrument to teach about his character and point others to him through her story.

Scripture portrays God's patient nature in his interaction with Sarah. God is slow to anger and abounds in faithful love and truth (Ps. 86:15). Thankfully, Sarah's unbelief did not turn his purposes aside.[7] Sarah had been looking to her circumstances rather than her God. In God's words, "Is anything impossible for the LORD?" (Gen. 18:14), he directs Sarah past her hopeless circumstances and toward him.[8] There isn't any problem in your life or difficulty you face that is too hard for the sovereign Lord. God can turn your unbelief into faith.

We can learn from Sarah's mistake by remembering that God is good, even when our circumstances are not. God's nature is such that when we face troubles, he wants us to see him beyond the fog and realize he is right in the middle of it. I always try to remind myself that when something happens that surprises me, it is never a surprise to God and is part of his ultimate plan. He still sits on his throne in the midst of my troubles. Not only that, but he is also looking tenderly down to me hoping I'll remember he is there. In Genesis 21, we'll see that God eventually granted Sarah the gift of Isaac. This time she laughed again, but her laughter had changed from scorn to joy and delirious wonder at God's goodness.[9]

Even when our circumstances are not what we planned, God should still receive our trust because his plans are always better. Give Jesus the wheel of your circumstances. Call him in your time of need; he will show up. God's blessing is waiting for you at the end of releasing control.

REFLECTION

In what area of your life have you grasped onto control instead of fully releasing it to God?

What would it look like, this week, to practically give that area over to God?

PRAYER

Faithful Creator, I recognize that since you created everything, any control I think I have is just an illusion because you are sovereign. I confess that I hold on too tightly to my illusion of control and don't trust your sovereignty. I give you complete control of my life because I know and trust that you know what you are doing, and I trust your will for my life.

Humility and Vulnerability

Genesis 18:2, 15, 27; 2 Corinthians 6:11–13

Our four moves during the first three years of marriage and my husband's frequent deployments made a difficult beginning to married life. I was overcome with sorrow and loneliness. It seemed like I would just start to form a friendship, and then we'd move again. After six months of desperate loneliness, I further resolved to avoid these periods of isolation. So I put on my big-girl pants and got brave. I pushed past my insecurities and uncomfortableness. I opened myself up quickly to others and jumped headfirst into vulnerability with prospective friends. To minimize my risk, I prayed about whom to expose myself to before plunging into vulnerability with new acquaintances. Thankfully, God never allowed a person to burn me, and I learned that others also longed for relationship.

When Abraham saw the three men, he ran to meet them and bowed to the earth. There were different modes of bowing in Bible times, ranging from bowing the head to bending the knees to prostrating before someone. The Hebrew phrase for "bowed down" in Genesis 18:2, *vaiyishtachu*, indicates Abraham exercised the most extreme form of reverence before these strangers.[1] He prostrated himself before his guests with respect, reverence, and humility.

Sarah gave us a poor example of humility and vulnerability when she ridiculously tried to hide her laughter and lack of faith in God by denying it. God confronted her, some say, not because he wanted her to feel bad but because he wanted her to be authentic and transparent about her fears.[2] She resisted vulnerability, and it caused adverse consequences for her.

In verse 27, Abraham spoke of himself as just dust and ashes. This term "dust" is used by Job sixteen times in his book and associates him with lowliness and humility.[3] When Job repented in dust and ashes, he did so in utter humbleness.[4] Ezekiel also used the term in Ezekiel 27:30 associated with bitter crying and meekness.

Abraham exemplified humility and vulnerability with God, while Sarah did not. These examples teach us how to move toward deeper relationships with others. In 2 Corinthians 6:11–13, Paul said, "We have spoken openly to you, Corinthians; our heart has been opened wide. We are not withholding our affection from you, but you are withholding yours from us. I speak as to my children; as a proper response, open your heart to us." Paul set the example of no hidden agenda with the Corinthians.[5] Paul yearned for the Corinthians to be as open and loving toward him as he had been with them.[6] Paul encouraged the Corinthians to be authentic with him because he had been vulnerable with them.

The word *vulnerability* has its root in the military.[7] Vulnerable is derived from the Latin noun *vulnus*, which means "wound." Vulnerable originally meant capable of being physically wounded.[8] When a city's walls were strong and fortified, there was no fear of the enemy getting through. But when any part of the walls became vulnerable, the city's residents would likely suffer harm.[9]

Vulnerability is the willingness to open yourself up to another person to the point that there is a risk of being emotionally wounded.[10] This type of relationship moves past superficial relationships to real friendships. In the connection, you are sharing how you feel about something and are exposing yourself to risk.

We can be vulnerable with one another and pursue deep relationships. To do so, we must lower our protective walls and risk rejection. Deep friendships require openness.[11] When you open your life, others are encouraged to do the same and friendship can bloom.

The Bible is the story of God's desire for a relationship with us and for us to be in a relationship with others. God created us with a high need to be known by him and others here on earth.[12]

We can avoid the risk of opening ourselves up to potential harm. One researcher states: "Through my research, I found that vulnerability is the glue that holds relationships together. It is the magic sauce."[13] This same researcher also says: "Society has taught us that vulnerability is synonymous with weakness—but it's the opposite. Vulnerability is the willingness to show up and be seen by others in the face of uncertain outcomes."[14] Chuck Swindoll had similar thoughts when he said, "If we want the advantages of love, then we must be willing to take the risks of love, which require vulnerability. Of course, we can refuse this path and trod another one devoid of openness. But the toll on such a road is extremely high."[15]

Avoiding vulnerability results in avoiding intimate relationships. Refusing to go deep and staying superficial keeps us in loneliness and isolation.[16] As a military wife, you might feel like self-isolating. Resist this! You need other people. Take the risk, open yourself up, and recognize that vulnerability will blossom true friendships.

REFLECTION

Have you experienced that forming a solid friendship at each new duty location can take several months? How can you reduce that time and increase vulnerability? What could you do this week to extend an invitation to another military wife that could result in an authentic relationship?

Think of a current close relationship in your life. How do you feel you reflect God's love in that relationship?

PRAYER

God of Love, enable me to balance protecting myself from hurt with being willing to open up and form meaningful friendships quickly. In your sovereignty, protect me from harm by preventing me from exposing my true self to those who would take advantage of me. Guide me to the right people at each location and help me be sensitive to your leading on whom I should approach for genuine friendship.

Intercession

Genesis 18:22–33; 1 Timothy 2:1

During the two years our family was stationed in South Korea, my five-year-old son got a bug vacuum for his birthday. In April, it's not warm, and there are no visual signs of spring. After piling on coats, hats, and gloves, we ventured outside to search the playground and surrounding areas for unsuspecting bugs.

Korea is an urban society since there is limited land mass and much of the country is mountainous. Suburban neighborhoods don't exist, and families of all sizes live in high-rise apartment buildings with plastic playscapes just outside the building with padded cushioning and rare grass. A luxury would be a bit of sand and a tree or two. The country does have dedicated nature preserves in each city or town, but most of the playgrounds are rather barren.

We searched high and low for insects but found none. Before returning upstairs, the Holy Spirit compelled me to grab my kids' hands and intercede for the Creator to show us at least one bug so we could inspect and enjoy his creation.

Right after prayer, I felt induced to look into the lone tree next to the playground. My two preschoolers' eyes sparkled with amazement as we realized God had blanketed the tree with ladybugs. God can "do above and beyond all that we ask or think" (Eph. 3:20). God cares about all of the details of our lives, no matter how small they seem. Further than that, he expects believers to engage in intercessory prayer (1 Tim. 2:1).

Abraham knew the power and responsibility of intercessory prayer. The thought of those about to be destroyed burdened Abraham and caused him to mediate for them. I wonder if we are as worried for the people we know who are also about to be destroyed. Not only did Abraham concern himself with his lost neighbors, but he felt responsible for petitioning the Lord on their behalf.

Remarkably, the sovereign and almighty God allowed Abraham to petition him on behalf of his wretched neighbors.[1] Abraham's petitions can teach us three great principles about prayer.

First, prayer ought to be humble. As part of his prayer, Abraham spoke the humble phrase, "even though I am dust and ashes" (Gen. 18:27). Abraham didn't demand knowledge from God on his purposes in destroying the inhabitants of Sodom and Gomorrah.[2] He didn't seek to judge them or to judge God's conclusion regarding them. Nor did he presume to be able to tell God what to do. He knew he was lower than God and acknowledged such by appealing to the Lord as the one in authority.

Second, prayer ought to be persistent. In Abraham's conversation with God, he persisted in uttering his requests.[3] He didn't stop after a couple of requests but repeated his intercession six times on behalf of any righteous people in Sodom and Gomorrah.

Third, prayer ought to be motivated by God's glory. Abraham was wise to appeal to God's own character and glory.[4] Abraham was jealous for God's honor and thus argued that if the righteous perished with the guilty, this might mar God's integrity in the minds of men.[5] Moses used a similar tactic when petitioning God not to bring disaster upon the Israelites in Exodus 32.

Abraham knew his responsibility to intercede for his neighbors; we sometimes neglect that responsibility. Jesus has given us the ministry of authoritative prayer and the ability to bind Satan in his name.[6] We might not be able to welcome a visit from the Lord the way that Abraham did, but we can enter his holy presence through the blood of Jesus (not to mention his presence lives *in* us through the Holy Spirit's indwelling). The time is drawing near when Jesus will return, and he will judge all men just like the inhabitants of Sodom and Gomorrah.[7] We can avoid indifference to the doom of our friends and neighbors around us because they need to hear the good news. We have the privilege to present it to them![8]

Prayer is simply talking to God; there is no magic formula. Prayer does not have to be eloquent with high and lofty words.

Whether it's about the distressing parts of military life, your spouse's safety while serving the military, a struggle with our kids, a financial situation, or the salvation of a friend, God wants us to share our hearts and grow closer to him. When we neglect prayer, it's like we are not talking to a good friend; after time, the friendship won't be as close. The Lord desperately longs to be close to you. Max Lucado says, "Our prayers may be awkward. Our attempts may be feeble. But since the power of prayer is in the one who hears it and not in the one who says it, our prayers do make a difference."[9]

Additionally, we can have confidence when we pray. Richard Trench summarized this perspective: "Prayer is not overcoming God's reluctance but laying hold of his willingness."[10] There is so much untapped potential, yet we leave it when we fail to pray to God. John Piper concludes: "Prayer causes things to happen that wouldn't happen if you didn't pray."[11]

REFLECTION

Which area of prayer can you grow the most in and why: humility, persistence, or the motivation of God's glory?

Consider how you might lay hold of God's willingness to answer prayer: Who in your sphere of influence is in danger because they do not trust the Savior? Pray consistently for them and ask God to give you the opportunity to share the good news with them.

PRAYER

El Shama (the God Who Hears), thank you that Psalm 145 tells us that you are near to those who call on you in prayer. Allow me to long for a relationship with you and be willing to consistently come to you in prayer for my needs and also for the souls of the lost. When I am weak, enable me to persist in prayer and humbly present my requests to you.

Salty

Genesis 19:1–29; Luke 9:62

When your husband went to basic training, or its equivalent, his training probably involved bravely navigating an intense obstacle course. The training included a rope climb, climbing over a wall, crawling under obstacles, navigating water features, and traversing through mud. Can you imagine what would happen if your husband tried to navigate the obstacle course with his attention diverted and his gaze behind him at his barracks the whole time? This foolish behavior likely would have led to him being sent home from basic training early. At the very least, he would been yelled at by his military training officer and granted extra push-ups. In the real world, this lack of focus on his assignment would lead to mission failure and possibly death of him or his compatriots in his unit.

In this section of Genesis, because of the Lord's compassion (19:16), God sent angels to grab Lot's hands and force him and his family out of Sodom and Gomorrah before the city was destroyed. In verse 17, the angels instructed them to feverishly run for the lives and not look back or stop along the way. As the sulfur rained down to demolish Sodom and Gomorrah, Lot's wife looked back and became a pillar of salt (Gen. 19:26).

As a reminder, Lot's neighbors were wicked—not even ten righteous people could be found in the city. When they moved next to Sodom and Gomorrah, it doesn't seem like Lot and his wife influenced those around them toward faith in the Lord. Lot and his wife could have chosen to be on mission and be salt that would preserve those around them. Instead of being salt, his wife turned to salt.

It wasn't just Lot's wife's physical posture that resulted in her being turned to salt; more importantly, it was her heart posture. She was gazing, yearningly to return to what she had left. Rather than engaging in surviving, she was trying to move backward toward the comfort and security of her past life.

Have you ever wondered why Lot's wife was turned specifically into a pillar of salt? This wasn't God's usual form of judgment. In the days before refrigeration, salt kept meat or fish from decaying and preserved its goodness. Luke 17:32–33 helps interpret: "Remember Lot's wife! Whoever tries to make his life secure will lose it, and whoever loses his life will preserve it." Instead of trying to impact and save those around her, Lot's wife was worried about preserving her own life and belongings.

The teaching about Lot's wife looking back is similar to the teaching of Luke 9:62, where Jesus instructed that "No one who puts his hand to the plow and looks back is fit for the kingdom of God." Lot's wife was looking backward and was not focused on what God wanted her to do. Just like a farmer is called to protect his crop by focusing on his plowing, we are called to focus on the crop of the souls of men. Jesus gave similar instructions about losing your life in John 12:25 and parallel passages in Matthew and Luke.

We can learn from Lot's wife's error, that we need to be useful for the kingdom. Don't be like Lot's wife; focus on the Lord. This involves being salt to those around you wherever the Lord takes you in your military adventure. It also involves getting behind your man, keeping your hand on the plow of discipleship, and allowing your husband to lead you boldly as you serve your military community and other neighbors. Now that you are married to a military man, embrace it as an opportunity to meet many people who need some seasoning with salt and make an eternal difference in their lives.

The Lord also opened my eyes to see that serving in uniform was more than just a job but a special calling. My husband saw his military career as a mission, and I could choose to join him on a mission to reach and serve the military and their families in our midst.

Each military base was then a mission field. We were to spread salt to those God put us in contact with to preserve them. God transformed my perspective to see my husband's calling to serve the military as a joint calling to extend Christian hospitality and shake some salt on our fellow military friends. We could serve the Lord just like missionaries, but while serving on active duty.

Our family embraced the opportunity to be the hands and feet of Jesus to the families in our unit. God had given us this opportunity to put others' interests above our own and to speak life to others. I formed many relationships during that time that moved to spiritual conversations and mentorship with spouses of military members.

As we continued moving, we kept hosting small groups in our home to invest spiritually to those in our midst. My support enabled my husband to influence those serving in uniform too. I no longer saw my husband's calling to serve the military as just his job; it was now a joint mission for the Lord.

A calling is defined as "a strong inner impulse toward a particular course of action or work which usually involves helping people and may be accompanied by a conviction of divine influence."[1] If you don't think God has given you a calling to live on mission, I want to challenge you. Eric Liddell said boldly, "We are all missionaries. Wherever we go, we either bring people nearer to Christ or repel them from Christ."[2] So you don't have the option to influence people in some way toward Christ.

You are not married to someone serving in the military by accident. If God placed you in this military marriage, he wants you to be on a mission to serve God wherever your feet land. Keep your eyes focused on making disciples, not looking back. Pick up the saltshaker! Here are a few practical tips that will help you embrace a mission mentality:

- **Have a positive attitude.** You can choose to be miserable in any assignment, but you can also choose to see it as an opportunity. Often the most significant relationships form in the most remote communities.
- **Recognize you are not in control; God is.**
- **Embrace the hard.** The military lifestyle is fertile ground for spiritual transformation in your life and those around you.
- **Look for ways to be involved in the military community where God has placed you.**
- **Manage expectations.** Your spouse wants to be home for all the events and dinners, but sometimes a duty to nation gets in the way. Lower your expectations and be pleasantly surprised when he can be home.
- **Pray for your spouse and your marriage.** Satan will try to divide you. Recognize this and pray against it and for the protection of your commitment to one another.

REFLECTION

Do you sometimes feel like you are in your husband's shadow, supporting him in his calling but not sharing his passion? Why or why not?

What one practical thing can you or you and your husband do to reach the military in your midst and spread some preserving salt around you?

PRAYER

Judge of All the Earth, help me see my responsibility to be like salt and influence those in my midst in the military. Enable me to catch a vision for what you would have me and my family practically do to be on mission for you while my husband is serving in the military.

God's Protection

Genesis 20:1–18

I'm grateful that God has allowed me to parent two children. We had wanted a larger family through birth or adoption. God never opened my womb again. We learned to trust his sovereignty even though we didn't quite understand why he closed the door to growing our family.

We attempted to adopt four times after our daughter. God closed the door on those. Eventually, God asked me to be content with what I had. Even though I didn't understand it at the time, God had something more extraordinary in mind. I've learned that a closed door from God may be his protection or his calling to something better.

My husband and I now serve full-time with a Christian ministry that works with the military on four military installations in our area. One of our areas of ministry is engaging with cadets at the Air Force Academy. Because of the discipleship and large group gathering for our ministry, we've formed relationships with hundreds of college-age kids, many of whom come to our home on the weekends and evenings to hang out or get counsel. God didn't open our home to adoption or other children because he had many spiritual children he wanted us to welcome. He knew if we brought home other kids, we probably wouldn't be doing what he has called us to do now.

After the destruction of Sodom and Gomorrah, Sarah and Abraham were faced with famine again.[1] Abraham had learned about the nature of God, but seemed to trust more in what he could see than what he could not. Abraham and Sarah moved south to Gerar, where a powerful king named Abimelech ruled the area. While we all wish Abraham would have learned his lesson about lying regarding his marriage, the Scriptures reveal that for a second time, Abraham feared for his life and played off Sarah as his sister and not his wife.[2]

It appears that Abraham thought he could keep Sarah from being taken into Abimelech's harem while saving his own life. He thought he could set Sarah's bride price high enough to keep Abimelech from being able to afford her.[3] Abraham was trying to protect Sarah in his own strength instead of trusting God.[4] But he had to let God protect her, and God did. God intervened to ensure the certain outcome of his promise to grant Sarah and Abraham a son.[5]

Interestingly, even the heathen king was more honorable than Abraham because as soon as he realized he had done wrong, he bent his knee to God and allowed Sarah and Abraham to be released.[6] Even though not a worshipper of Yahweh, Abimelech still had a strong reverence for God and an acute sense of right and wrong.[7]

I get so frustrated with Abraham when I read how he used the same false story with Abimelech that he had tried earlier with Pharaoh. After all he had been through with God, I want Genesis 20 to say something different at this juncture in his story. But then God reminds me that I mess up repeatedly too. One of the many reasons that I believe the Word is true is because it doesn't deny the mistakes of biblical characters.[8] We see imperfection in Abraham and other characters like David and Noah. Inconsistencies in the heroes of the faith remind me of the hopelessness of our original nature and how much we need God.[9]

So why did Abraham fall into this pattern of sin? He should have grown out of it by now. It had been about twenty years since his first failure in Egypt.[10] It seems probable that Abraham had not confessed and truly repented of that sin in Egypt. Maybe Abraham thought that sin wouldn't rise and trap him again.[11]

The other possibility is that Abraham's view of himself was a bit too lofty, and he thought he might not be able to fail in the same way again. Maybe he thought he could take care of Sarah without God's intervention.[12] Abraham had sinned by doubting God and taking matters into his own hands.[13]

Thankfully, God protected Sarah against her husband's bad ideas. The promise of the son, Isaac, could have been in dire jeopardy if God had not intervened. God showed Sarah and Abraham that he could maintain his covenant and secure the realization of his promise against all opposition from sinful desires.[14] God remains sovereign even when we doubt his ability to care for us.[15]

The only safe course for dealing with sin is to bring it to the light, confess it, and then receive spiritual cleansing.[16] First John 1:9 promises that as soon as it is confessed, we are cleansed of our sin and purified from all unrighteousness. When we refuse to forgive ourselves or stay frozen in a pit of shame, that is not God's will for us, but a ploy of the enemy, Satan. Shame is from the enemy and keeps us from moving forward in our walk with him.

Abraham's failure doesn't seem to have changed God's view of him. Not once in Abraham's journey did God refer to Abraham's past sin in a way to shame him by a memory of it.[17] To God, Abraham's mistake was forgiven and gone.[18] God remained gracious even when Abraham sinned.[19]

What a pleasure and opportunity we have to serve a God like this. In Christ, our God doesn't count our past sins against us. He protects us even when we mess up. He keeps his covenant no matter what we do. God allows us the opportunity to confess and be cleansed when we sin. God is always gracious.

Some circumstances you might be struggling with letting go of or trying to control include: carrying the weight of a past sin that keeps you burdened with guilt, an assignment for your husband you desperately wanted but you didn't get, or an assignment you wanted to avoid but were sent to anyway; a fulfilling job for yourself in your current location; having to deliver a baby without your husband by your side; that promotion your husband didn't get that you expected; or that deployment that is unavoidable.

REFLECTION

What circumstances has God protected you from that you didn't initially understand?

When you sin, how do you wholeheartedly confess and repent of that sin so that it doesn't become a sin pattern you repeat?

PRAYER

Great Protector, thank you for your abundant grace and compassion. When we fail, you don't let that failure define us but welcome us back with loving arms. When fearful circumstances come my way, let me remember your sovereignty and protection and not try to manage things in my own strength. Help me trust all the things that may happen in my husband's military career that seem outside our control but may be part of your divine plan.

God of the Impossible

Genesis 21:1–7; Job 42:2; Matthew 19:26; 1 Peter 1:7

But why, God?" I sobbed. I rocked myself from side to side as I cried out to the Lord for my daughter. Military-wife life had built character in me, and I'd been able to push through thirteen moves and multiple deployments. But this was different. This hardship seemed insurmountable. It wasn't my direct pain that ached, but the agony of watching my teenage daughter tumble in despair. After nine moves, all the resiliency that military kids possess seemed to have run out. She was cloaked with heaviness. A cloud of depression engulfed her. This move and the difficulty of making friends and other teen struggles seemed too much for her, and her emotions collapsed under adversity.

That day, I pushed myself to the installation chapel to join other military wives for our weekly Bible study. Although I was a mess, I knew I needed to surround myself with other women who could encourage me and point me to God. My confidence in God was running low, and I needed to borrow faith from my sisters in Christ. Although I wept through most of the study, the other women's insights on the study and prayers added fuel to my faith.

Like my situation with my daughter, Sarah faced a situation that seemed too hard for God. Nothing is too hard for God. Sarah became pregnant when she and Abraham were quite old; in fact, Scripture says they were past childbearing age in Genesis 18:11. There was no natural reason why Abraham and Sarah could have had a child at this age.[1] At the age of ninety, God gave Sarah the strength to conceive and bear a child. It happened at exactly the time God had said it would happen. God kept his promise. Given their age, it was indeed a sign of God's omnipotence. Genesis 21:7 indicates that God did another miracle because she could nurse the baby in her old age.[2] The author of Hebrews commended Sarah for her faith in God's ability to grant her the power to conceive. Graciously, God passed over the fact that Sarah had struggled with unbelief earlier in the story.[3]

Although Sarah had previously laughed in unbelief, now she displayed joyful laughter that honored God. Sarah led her community in exuberant chuckles of praise of what her God could do! I wonder if Sarah recalled her doubt about her ability to have a child when she had overheard the Lord telling Abraham that she would have a son the next year. God had rhetorically questioned, "Is anything impossible for the LORD?" in Genesis 18:14. Sarah could testify that nothing was outside of God's capabilities.

From the miraculous account of Isaac's birth, we learn five principal lessons about God:[4]

- **God is not in haste to work out his plans.** He always knows the perfect time to bring about his purposes. It may not be your agenda, but it will be the best itinerary.
- **Nothing can impede or prevent God's purpose.** No obstacle is too high for God. Remember, God possesses infinite power. God cannot be put in a box.
- **God is faithful.** You will have times when you are tempted to doubt. Borrow faith from your sisters in Christ and the Word of God to remind yourself of God's dependability. One of the reasons we can study the Bible is its accounts of God's faithfulness remind us he is able and reliable.
- **Faith is tested so that it might be shown to be genuine.** First Peter 1:7 reminds us that faith is proven genuine through fire by comparing our trials to the process of refining gold. In purifying gold, the refiner heats the fire so high that it causes the metal to melt into a liquid. The impurities rise to the top and are skimmed off to leave the precious metal in the pot. Just like the

gold-refining process, the heat of trials can reveal some impure character traits or doubt to the surface that need to be removed. This helps shape us into the person God wants us to be, who will better reflect his glory to his world. Each challenge I've faced has stretched and enlarged my faith. After a period of suffering, God gave my daughter a huge heart for ministry to his people and a passion for him that she would not have had if she had not been under the heat of hardship. Don't dash away from the refiner's fire! That fire creates a work of radiant beauty in you.

- **God has an established time and season for everything.** Guess what? Life's timing is not yours. Even when it doesn't seem like it, his timing is best. God maintains ultimate authority over every detail of your life. Chance and luck are not a reality with a sovereign God. God gave Sarah her promised son at the hour that he had appointed for Sarah and Abraham to have reached the mature faith they would need to continue God's purposes in their life.

Perhaps you read my story or look at Sarah's story and think your situation is different—your predicament is too hard for God. Matthew 19:26 tells us that Jesus said, "With man this is impossible, but with God all things are possible." When speaking of the Lord, Job said, "I know that you can do anything and no plan of yours can be thwarted" (Job 42:2). Your circumstance is not too hard for the Lord.

Military wives have to face some challenging situations. Maybe it is surviving the next deployment or dealing with your husband's sporadic shift-work schedule. It could be moving overseas. Or healing your husband from combat trauma or other invisible wounds of war. It might be handling some mental or physical health challenges yourself or with your children. No matter how serious you consider your problem to be—God can do it if he wills it. He is worthy of your full confidence.

REFLECTION

Do you have faithful friends who can lend you their belief when your confidence in God is running low? If not, how might you work toward finding some this week?

What situation seems too hard for God to intervene in? Tell these to God. Listen to what he says about his ability.

PRAYER

Controller of all things, help me to be like Job and believe that no purpose of yours can be thwarted. I'm struggling with circumstances that seem impossible. Give me strength, through your Spirit, to trust you are able to do anything. Help me learn what I need to through your refining fire and give me the strength not to run from you but press into you.

Prompt Obedience

Genesis 21:8–22; 17:23–26; 21:14; 22:3; John 14:15–16

I taught my kids "slow obedience is no obedience" and "obey all the way, right away." Primarily, I did this for safety reasons. I wanted to get an instant reaction if they were in danger without them questioning my request.

While stationed in Korea, my three-year-old daughter's immediate obedience saved her life. We were walking out of our apartment building to the community parking lot when she darted into the road. A car was approaching the parking lot from down the hill and couldn't see my daughter on the road due to the hill. Since she had been trained to obey, I yelled out for her to run back to me. Because she had been trained to stop immediately and come when I called her, her obedience got her out of the way of the speeding vehicle. She'd been trained not to question an authority that loved her and looked out for her welfare.

In less severe matters, immediate obedience also kept my kids from forgetting. I didn't like it when my kids told me they'd do something later because they would often forget what I originally asked. Honestly, *I'd* forget what I asked them to do sometimes! As adults, we forget that God has called us to the same level of obedience as we expect from our kids, or more.

In Genesis 21, we saw that God granted Sarah and Abraham a child exactly when he said he would. His word is reliable. Sarah and Abraham made some mistakes but learned that God was completely trustworthy. Although not perfect, Abraham's heart was that of an obedient follower of God. Sarah and Abraham show us a picture of the rewards of complete and prompt obedience, even when asked to do hard things. Abraham and Sarah started their journey with God when they obeyed God's request to leave their family and country (Gen. 12:4). God beckoned them to sacrifice all comfort to follow the call upon Abraham's life. There is no scriptural evidence that they asked for details of the land God was calling them to. They went because God requested it. Their faith fueled their obedience to God (Gen. 15:6).

When God told Abraham to circumcise himself and all the men in their camp, Abraham followed God; Sarah didn't stop him (Gen. 17:23). We see no hint of delay even though Abraham probably suspected it would be a painful procedure. There is no indication that Abraham or Sarah tried to talk God out of his command or sought counsel from others before submitting.

Abraham also obeyed God's instruction to listen to Sarah and send Ishmael away. Early the next morning, Abraham obeyed God (Gen. 21:14). It was likely difficult to follow since this meant sending away his firstborn son. Still, he trusted that God had to separate Ishmael to complete his plan for Isaac and the resulting nation. Abraham did not delay in following God's directions.

These other things God asked of Abraham were tough, but God had an even more challenging assignment for him—to sacrifice his son. Abraham did not drag his feet or return with more questions; there was no unbelief, just prompt obedience.[1] In Genesis 22:3, Abraham woke early in the morning and saddled his donkey to obey God's command with Isaac. If I'd have been Abraham, I might not have gone first thing the next morning!

Jesus told us that we will keep his commandments if we love him. Obeying God if we love him can seem overwhelming, but considering Jesus's exhortation in context, he provides the power to follow it. John 14:15–16 states: "If you love me, you will keep my commands. And I will ask the Father, and he will give you another Counselor to be with you forever." The Spirit gives power for obedience.

We cannot live the Christian life in our own strength. Galatians 3:3 cautions us not to attempt the Christian walk by the power of our flesh. As we walk in the Spirit, daily depending upon God, we can live a life pleasing to God (Gal. 5:16). Walking in the Spirit is a moment-by-moment lifestyle of dependence upon the Holy Spirit for his abundant resources.[2] To depend upon the Spirit, we need to practice spiritual breathing.[3]

Spiritual breathing is when we exhale by confessing sins and agreeing with God concerning our sins according to 1 John 1:9. We then thank God for his forgiveness and truly repent (or turn the other way) from sin in attitude and action. Next, we inhale by surrendering control of our life to Christ, consciously relying upon the Holy Spirit to fill us with his presence and power.[4]

This daily breathing helps us experience intimate dependence upon the Holy Spirit.[5] We wouldn't intentionally leave for a long day of travel without charging a cell phone because we'd run out of power. The same is true with our spiritual life. We must consciously confess and surrender and then ask for Holy Spirit empowerment for obedience.

As military wives, we also can be asked to do difficult things. We trust God even when we don't understand. Some of the difficult things you may endure as a result of being a military wife may include: watching the emotional pain of your children when their dad is deployed; reintegrating after a deployment since both you and your spouse have changed, at least temporarily; struggling to find a meaningful career with frequent moves, often to somewhat isolated conditions; coping with a spouse with Post Traumatic Stress Disorder (PTSD) or coping with secondary PTSD yourself; worrying over a spouse who serves in harm's way; and managing the amount of time you spend packing and unpacking.

Trusting God when you cannot see pleases the Lord; there are blessings for obedience (Gen. 22:18; Luke 11:28). We can obey when it feels impossible because we have the indwelling Holy Spirit.

Paul instructed Christians not to get drunk on wine but to be filled with the Spirit (Eph. 5:18). Paul was contrasting the difference between being under the influence of wine and being under the influence of the Spirit. The infiltrating power of the Holy Spirit enables us to do things we couldn't do in our strength—that's obedience.[6]

REFLECTION

Specifically, what hard thing associated with marriage or military life is God asking you to do to obey him?

How can you incorporate spiritual breathing as part of your daily routine?

PRAYER

Loving God, I want to obey you. Help me recognize that I cannot live obediently in my own strength. Assist me in spiritually breathing daily and tapping into your strength to show my love to you through obedience.

The Lord Will Provide

Genesis 22; Hebrews 11:17–19

During World War II, the evacuation of Dunkirk was a turning point in favor of the Allied troops. German forces had cut off communications and transportation, pushing 400,000 Allied forces into the north and a sliver of the French coast. It seemed inevitable that the Nazi troops would overtake France and easily cross the water to invade England. On this same day, Winston Churchill of Britain asked his nation to pray for three days.[1] Hitler halted the advance for two more days, allowing the Allied forces to prepare. Low clouds and rain further slowed Hitler's advance. Then as the British orchestrated their evacuation, the smoke emitted from German bombs protected the exit effort and kept it undetected for four days.[2] Aided by 800 to 1,200 small leisure and fishing crafts, the mission evacuated

338,000 troops.[3] God provided vital ingredients for the success, which included weather and carefully orchestrated details that protected the Allied forces.

Genesis 22 is one of the most challenging but rewarding chapters in Scripture to understand. It is inconceivable that God asked Abraham to sacrifice his son, Isaac. God "asked" Abraham but didn't require him to complete the sacrifice. This test was likely presented to purify Abraham's faith and point to God's provision of Jesus to die on Calvary in our place.

We don't understand the cultural context of child sacrifice for Abraham. Every religion, except Judaism, that Abraham would have seen at this point demanded child sacrifice, including the faith of the family he left in Ur.[4] So Abraham likely wouldn't have been surprised and would have just thought that now his God had similar requirements to the pagan gods.[5] Abraham eventually learned a valuable lesson to pass to his descendants that Yahweh is not like the other gods.[6]

God had promised Abraham that all future blessings, including the promise to bless all nations through the Savior, were to come through Isaac.[7] God had promised blessing through the son he was asking Abraham to kill.[8] Although Abraham didn't understand the solution to the difficulty, he obeyed because he had learned God possessed a trustworthy character.[9] Faith is believing God and acting upon it, which is precisely what Abraham did.[10]

God wanted Abraham to prove that he loved God more than the things of this life.[11] Due to the long wait for his son,

Abraham might have loved Isaac more than God.[12] God had to teach Abraham that he was to keep his attention on the One who performed the miracle instead of the outcome of the miracle.[13] So, although God didn't require the death of Isaac, he did require Abraham to die to himself.[14]

Abraham informed his servants that he and the boy would worship and return. Certainly, it was an act of worship that Abraham was willing to give up everything for God. Because of his faith in the God of the resurrection, Abraham said they would return.[15] Isaac had been born to Sarah when both Abraham and Sarah were incapable of having children. God had brought life out of death once. Abraham was convinced God could do it again.[16]

Abraham's near-sacrifice of Isaac is a picture of God's actual sacrifice. At the cross, God plunged the knife into his Son and Jesus willingly died for all who profess faith.[17] Someone had to die, but it wasn't Isaac. It was Jesus.

When Abraham placed the wood on Isaac's shoulders, this was a prophetic image of Jesus, who would eventually carry the wooden cross to the place of the skull.[18] Isaac went willingly with his father because he trusted him; Jesus went willingly for the same reason.[19] Both Abraham and God are loving fathers. In order to save Isaac, God provided a ram caught in the thicket; in order to save us, God provided himself.[20] The mountain where God asked Abraham to go and offer Isaac was Mount Moriah. The Jews eventually built the temple in this spot. This location is where the Jews offered animal sacrifices and served as the site of the crucifixion of the ultimate sacrifice, Jesus.[21]

Abraham named the place Jehovah Jireh, which means "the Lord will provide," to remind him of God's deliverance. This Hebrew word *Jireh*, is a form of the verb *ra'ah*, which means "God himself will see to it."[22] This name was pointing to his own experience but also beyond it to the future. In Abraham's most significant moment of need, God was telling him he was there. He'd not left his side and would provide for his needs.[23]

Understanding the implications of the linkage between Abraham's offering of Isaac and the sacrifice of Jesus is a significant part of the Bible's message. Redemption has always been the central theme of God's Word. The death of Jesus bought redemption. To receive that redemption, you must place your faith in his sacrifice on your behalf and put your life under his authority.

God sees our significant problem of sin, but he also sees our minor issues. The God who provided for the perfect sacrifice continues to be the God who will provide for his people.[24] Jehovah Jireh will see to your needs. God sees your problems and will provide for that assignment or orders you are waiting on. God will provide for your basic needs when your husband is deployed. He will provide your kids with the right school environment and friends in your next duty station. God may not orchestrate the plan as you think it should go, but he will provide wherever and whenever he takes you and your family on this journey with the military.

REFLECTION

Have you truly accepted Christ's sacrifice on your behalf? Does your life show evidence of being under his authority?

What things are you struggling to trust that God will provide for you?

PRAYER

Jehovah Jireh, thank you for providing Jesus to die in my place and for your plan of redemption. Thank you that you aren't like false gods because you are so much greater than them. Enable me to trust you and not rely upon things of this world but only on you, Lord.

Ending Well

Genesis 23; Isaiah 51:1–2; Philippians 1:21;
Hebrews 11:11; 1 Peter 3:3–6

There was always a possibility that my military husband wouldn't make it home from a deployment or training mission. Recognizing the sovereignty of God doesn't mean that he promises that your husband will come home. The possibility of death is real for military wives. Unless Jesus returns first, we will all face death.

Inspired by the Holy Spirit, Paul was able to dispel the innate fear of death. Paul learned that "to live is Christ and to die is gain" (Phil. 1:21). Paul knew that to keep living would benefit the believers but not prove better for him personally. Paul knew that death was not the ending, but the actual beginning.

Charles Spurgeon, one of history's most renowned Christian preachers, died suddenly at fifty-seven from rapid kidney failure. Spurgeon's writing says he was prepared for and anticipated his eventual home. Spurgeon said, "The best moment of a Christian's life is his last one because it is the one nearest heaven." He also said, "It is not a loss to die; it is a lasting, perpetual gain."[1] C. S. Lewis brushed beauty on this concept in his Chronicles of Narnia, describing death as the "beginning of the real story."[2]

What did Sarah teach us about eternity as she finished her life? What does God say of Sarah?

Sarah and Abraham's lives were intricately woven together. Abraham founded Judaism, and the Bible writers hailed him for his exemplary faith. Abraham could likely not have become such a spiritual giant if he had not had Sarah by his side.[3] You, too, have an essential role to serve beside your warrior.

Like you, Sarah had to fight massive waves of doubt, fear, and uncertainty. Sarah is heralded for her faith and praised as a godly model in both the Old and New Testaments. Isaiah 51 instructs us to look to Sarah's example of pursuing righteousness and seeking the Lord. Sarah was far from perfect, and God didn't judge her solely during her moments of weakness. Even though she had flaws, she always found her way to seek the Lord.

As we've explored already, Peter spoke of Sarah as holy and commended her for not giving way to fear after allowing her husband to lead (1 Pet. 3:5–6). Sarah didn't allow fear to rule her. She didn't give way to terror because she held firm to the promises of God and looked to the pledged future.

Sarah eventually realized that God would keep his promises and developed an unshakable faith which caused her to be listed as a hero of the faith by the writer of Hebrews. Sarah is the only wife listed in Hebrews 11. Sarah had chosen to leave her home and father's home to accompany Abraham on his calling. She cheered Abraham through his troubles and upheld him through life's disappointments. She faithfully stood by Abraham.

Abraham showed how much he valued Sarah when he purchased from the Hittites the only land he would ever own to bury her body. Abraham had been offered the land for free, but the four hundred shekels he paid was more than its worth.[4] Abraham paid such a price because he wanted to honor Sarah but also because he trusted God's promise. Abraham buying the small spot of land was an act of confidence in God's promise concerning the land.[5]

Even though God had promised Abraham the entire land of Canaan, he only owned the property where he buried Sarah. Hebrews 11:9–10 tells us that Abraham was willing to be content living in tents because he was looking for a city whose architect and builder is God. Abraham focused on where he would spend eternity. Although not stated explicitly, Abraham shared Paul's perspective of heaven being a gain. Both Abraham and Sarah knew they were not home because in the presence of God was home.

As you reflect on the life of Sarah, are you, like Spurgeon, prepared for death? What about your friend or neighbor? Death is a reality for each of us, but if you have accepted Christ, you have nothing to fear. There are friends God has put in your path that might not yet believe and submit to his lordship. God has a mission for you, and it's the assignment he gave to his followers in Matthew 28:19–20: "Go . . . and make disciples . . . teaching them to observe everything I have commanded you. . . . I am with you always." The word *go* is a command and indicates an ongoing action. Don't just go, keep going.

We are responsible for taking what we've learned and passing it along to others. We don't stop at evangelizing; we stand alongside those we share with and make disciples. Jesus created disciples by doing life with them and teaching them along the way. We make disciples by standing side by side with others as we walk together in our journey of spiritual growth. Do you have the faith to believe that you've been placed in the exact places you will live at the precise times for "such a time as this"? And yet, we do not live for this life alone. God wants you in the path of people who need to understand that eternity is our great hope. When we pass from this life, indeed, we will have just begun to live.

REFLECTION

Whom might God have placed in your life to invest in as a disciple?

How can you keep a perspective that this is not your home and the troubles of this life are only temporary?

PRAYER

Great Overcomer, thank you that I have nothing to fear in death. Because of Christ, I know that my true home is a much better place. Empower me to be boldly on a mission to bring my friends and loved ones to your kingdom.

Notes

INTRODUCTION

1. Paul Wegner, "Genesis," S1112–11, Old Testament Introduction I, Los Angeles, CA, September 14 and 21, 2021.

2. *Merriam-Webster Dictionary*, s.v. "calling," accessed May 10, 2023, https://www.merriam-webster.com/dictionary/calling?utm_campaign =sd&utm_medium=serp&utm_source=jsonld.

DAY 1

1. Paul Wegner, "Genesis," S1112–11, Old Testament Introduction I, Los Angeles, CA, September 14 and 21, 2021.

2. *Brown-Driver-Briggs Concordance,* s.v. "El Shaddai," accessed November 18, 2023, https://biblehub.com/hebrew/7706.htm.

DAY 2

1. *Old Testament Hebrew Lexicon*, s.v. "dabaq," accessed November 18, 2023, https://www.biblestudytools.com/lexicons/hebrew/kjv/dabaq .html.

2. "Cleave," dabhand.org, accessed March 31, 2023, http://www .dabhand.org/Word%20Studies/Cleave.htm.

3. "What Is Forge Welding: A Comprehensive Beginner's Guide," Makeitfrommetal.com, accessed May 10, 2023, https://makeitfrommetal .com/what-is-forge-welding-a-comprehensive-beginners-guide/.

4. "Welding Myths Part 3: A Weld Is Never as Strong as the Parent Material," Joiningtech.com, accessed May 10, 2023, https://joiningtech .com/welding_myths_3/.

DAY 3

1. Andrew E. Hill and John H. Walton, *A Survey of the Old Testament* (Grand Rapids: Zondervan, 2009), 49.

2. Paul Wegner, "Genesis," S1112–11, Old Testament Introduction I, Los Angeles, CA, September 14 and 21, 2021.

3. Ralph D. Winter, "The Kingdom Strikes Back," in *Perspectives on the World Christian Movement: A Reader*, eds. Ralph D. Winter and Steven C. Hawthorne (Pasadena, CA: William Carey Library, 2009), 209–27.

DAY 4

1. Family Life Weekend to Remember Conference, "Session 8–Women to Women: Embracing God's Wonderful Design" (Newport, RI, March 8–10, 2013), 89.

2. "What Does 'a Suitable Helper' Mean?" Wordimpartation.com, October 25, 2019, https://wordimpartation.com/what-does-a-suitable-helper-mean/.

3. Michael Rydelnik and Michael Vanlaningham, eds., *The Moody Bible Commentary* (Chicago: Moody Publishers, 2014), 1854.

4. John Piper, "A Metaphor of Christ and the Church," Desiring God, accessed November 18, 2023, https://www.desiringgod.org/articles/a-metaphor-of-christ-and-the-church.

DAY 5

1. Marty Soloman and Brent Billings, "Letting Go," November 16, 2016, BEMA Podcast 9 audio, 40 mins 49 secs, https://www.bemadiscipleship.com/9.

2. T. Desmond Alexander, "Genesis 11:2–4," *ESV Study Bible* (Wheaton, IL: Crossway, 2008), 69.

3. Soloman and Billings, "Letting Go," November 16, 2016.

4. Soloman and Billings, "Letting Go," November 16, 2016.

5. Soloman and Billings, "Letting Go," November 16, 2016.

DAY 6

1. "What Does It Mean to Call Upon the Name of the Lord?," GotQuestions.org, accessed February 15, 2023, https://www.got questions.org/call-upon-the-name-of-the-Lord.html.

2. Ray VanderLaan, "City Gates in the Bible," *That the World May Know*, accessed November 18, 2023, https://www.thattheworldmayknow .com/city-gates-in-the-bible.

DAY 7

1. Christopher Chabris and Daniel Simons, *The Invisible Gorilla: And Other Ways Our Intuitions Deceive Us* (New York: Broadway Paperbacks, 2009).

2. Theodore H. Epp, *The God of Abraham, Isaac, and Jacob* (Lincoln, NE: Back to the Bible, 1970), 50–51.

3. Epp, *The God of Abraham, Isaac, and Jacob*, 50–51.

4. Epp, *The God of Abraham, Isaac, and Jacob*, 50–51.

5. Epp, *The God of Abraham, Isaac, and Jacob*, 50–51.

6. Epp, *The God of Abraham, Isaac, and Jacob*, 50–51.

7. Epp, *The God of Abraham, Isaac, and Jacob*, 51, 54–55.

8. Marty Soloman and Brent Billings, "Letting Go," November 16, 2016, in BEMA Podcast 9 audio, 40 mins 49 secs, https://www.bema discipleship.com/9.

9. Epp, *The God of Abraham, Isaac, and Jacob*, 51, 54–55.

DAY 8

1. Timothy Keller, *Center Church: Doing Balanced Gospel Ministry in Your City* (Grand Rapids: Zondervan, 2021), 34.

2. Theodore H. Epp, *The God of Abraham, Isaac, and Jacob* (Lincoln, NE: Back to the Bible, 1970), 57.

3. Epp, *The God of Abraham, Isaac, and Jacob*, 44–47.

DAY 9

1. Theodore H. Epp, *The God of Abraham, Isaac, and Jacob* (Lincoln, NE: Back to the Bible, 1970), 65.

2. Epp, *The God of Abraham, Isaac, and Jacob*, 65.

3. Epp, *The God of Abraham, Isaac, and Jacob*, 65.

4. Dan Rickett, "Biblical Views: Safeguarding Abraham," *Biblical Archaeological Society Library*, January/February 2019, https://library .biblicalarchaeology.org/department/biblical-views-safeguarding -abraham/.

DAY 10

1. "What Does It Mean to Call Upon the Name of the Lord?," GotQuestions.org, accessed March 9, 2023, https://www.gotquestions .org/call-upon-the-name-of-the-Lord.html.

2. "Midrash Tanchuma," *Sefaria: A Living Library of Torah*, accessed January 15, 2023, https://www.sefaria.org/Midrash_Tanchuma %2C_Lech_Lecha.5.2?ven=Midrash_Tanhuma-.

3. "Ancient Mesopotamia Warfare—Weapons," psu.edu, accessed November 18, 2023, https://sites.psu.edu/ancientmesopotamianwarfare/.

4. Michael Nott, "Psalm 91: The Soldier's Psalm," Military Christian Fellowship of Australia, May 24, 2016, https://mcf-a.org.au/articles/the -soldiers-psalm/.

5. "Psalm 91 Cards," accessed May 10, 2023, https://thefathers business.com/product/psalm-91-cards/.

6. "7 Powerful Prayers for Soldiers," accessed May 15, 2023, https:// prayforeverything.com/powerful-prayers-for-soldiers/.

DAY 11

1. Theodore H. Epp, *The God of Abraham, Isaac, and Jacob* (Lincoln, NE: Back to the Bible, 1970), 82–83.

2. T. Desmond Alexander, "Genesis 14:18," *ESV Study Bible* (Wheaton, IL: Crossway, 2008), 76.

3. Epp, *The God of Abraham, Isaac, and Jacob*, 82–83.

4. Epp, *The God of Abraham, Isaac, and Jacob*, 82–83.

5. Marty Soloman and Brent Billings, "Walking the Blood Path," December 1, 2016, BEMA Podcast 10 audio, 49 mins 49 secs, https://www.bemadiscipleship.com/10.

6. James Montgomery Boice, *Genesis: An Expositional Commentary*, vol. 2 (Grand Rapids: Zondervan, 1985), 82.

7. Billy Graham, *The Journey: Living by Faith in an Uncertain World* (Nashville: Thomas Nelson, 2007), 242.

DAY 12

1. Max Lucado, *Fearless: Imagine Your Life Without Fear* (Nashville: Thomas Nelson, 2009), 74.

2. Theodore H. Epp, *The God of Abraham, Isaac, and Jacob* (Lincoln, NE: Back to the Bible, 1970), 85–86.

3. Nancy Guthrie, *The One Year Book of Discovering Jesus in the Old Testament* (Carol Stream, IL: Tyndale House Publishers, Inc., 2010), February 9.

4. Guthrie, *The One Year Book of Discovering Jesus in the Old Testament*, February 9.

5. Guthrie, *The One Year Book of Discovering Jesus in the Old Testament*, February 9.

6. James Montgomery Boice, *Genesis: An Expositional Commentary*, vol. 2 (Grand Rapids: Zondervan, 1985), 90–91.

DAY 13

1. Travis Hastings, "Patience Produces Pearls" (sermon, Cross Fellowship Church, April 29, 2023).

2. Theodore H. Epp, *The God of Abraham, Isaac, and Jacob* (Lincoln, NE: Back to the Bible, 1970), 88–90.

3. Epp, *The God of Abraham, Isaac, and Jacob*, 88–90.

DAY 14

1. G. K. Chesterton, *Autobiography* (London: Hutchinson and Co., 1936), 141.

2. Michael Rydelnik and Michael Vanlaningham, eds., *The Moody Bible Commentary* (Chicago: Moody Publishers, 2014), 72.

3. *Strong's Concordance*, s.v. "aman," accessed May 10, 2023, https://biblehub.com/lexicon/genesis/15-6.htm.

4. Warren W. Wiersbe, *The Wiersbe Bible Commentary: Old Testament* (Colorado Springs: David C. Cook, 2007), 68.

5. James Montgomery Boice, *Genesis: An Expositional Commentary*, vol. 2 (Grand Rapids: Zondervan, 1985), 98–103.

6. Boice, *Genesis*, 98–103.

7. Nancy Guthrie, *The One Year Book of Discovering Jesus in the Old Testament* (Carol Stream, IL: Tyndale House Publishers, Inc., 2010), February 10–11.

8. Boice, *Genesis*, 98–103.

9. Boice, *Genesis*, 98–103.

10. Guthrie, *The One Year Book of Discovering Jesus in the Old Testament*, February 10–11.

DAY 15

1. Dennis Rainey, "Ashley and Michael's Covenant," Family Life, accessed March 15, 2023, https://www.familylife.com/articles/topics/marriage/getting-married/engagements-and-weddings/ashley-and-michaels-covenant/#.VNLA3dJ4pcQ.

2. John Piper, "Marriage: God's Showcase of Covenant-Keeping Grace," Desiring God, February 11, 2007, https://www.desiringgod.org/messages/marriage-gods-showcase-of-covenant-keeping-grace.

3. Piper, "Marriage: God's Showcase of Covenant Keeping Grace."

4. Paul Wegner, "Genesis," S1112–11, Old Testament Introduction I, Los Angeles, CA, September 14 and 21, 2021.

5. Nancy Guthrie, *The One Year Book of Discovering Jesus in the Old Testament* (Carol Stream, IL: Tyndale House Publishers, Inc., 2010), February 12.

6. Guthrie, *The One Year Book of Discovering Jesus in the Old Testament*, February 12.

7. James Montgomery Boice, *Genesis: An Expositional Commentary*, vol. 2 (Grand Rapids: Zondervan, 1985), 116–21.

8. Guthrie, *The One Year Book of Discovering Jesus in the Old Testament*, February 12.

9. Boice, *Genesis*, 116–21.

10. Boice, *Genesis*, 116–21.

11. Marty Soloman and Brent Billings, "Walking the Blood Path," December 1, 2016, in BEMA Podcast 10 audio, 49 mins 49 secs, https://www.bemadiscipleship.com/10.

12. Soloman and Billings, "Walking the Blood Path."

13. Soloman and Billings, "Walking the Blood Path."

14. Boice, *Genesis*, 116–21.

15. Piper, "Marriage: God's Showcase of Covenant Keeping Grace."

DAY 16

1. "Two Headed Snakes—Do They Exist? Everything You Need to Know," The Reptarium, accessed January 28, 2023, https://thereptarium.com/pages/ben-jerry-2-headed-california-kingsnake.

2. "Two Headed Snakes."

3. Nancy Demoss Wolgemuth, "Two Hearts Aren't Better Than One," *Revive Our Hearts*, January 29, 2008, https://www.reviveourhearts.com/podcast/revive-our-hearts/two-heads-aren-t-better-than-one/.

4. Wolgemuth, "Two Hearts Aren't Better Than One."

5. Kimberly Wagner, *Fierce Women: The Power of a Soft Warrior* (Chicago: Moody Publishers, 2012), 10.

6. Wagner, *Fierce Women*, 11.

7. Wagner, *Fierce Women*, 26.

DAY 17

1. James Montgomery Boice, *Genesis: An Expositional Commentary,* vol. 2 (Grand Rapids: Zondervan, 1985), 125–27.

2. Paul Wegner, "Genesis," S1112–11, Old Testament Introduction I, Los Angeles, CA, September 14 and 21, 2021.

3. Wegner, "Genesis."

4. Boice, *Genesis*, 122–27.

5. Boice, *Genesis*, 122–27.

6. Michael Rydelnik and Michael Vanlaningham, eds., *The Moody Bible Commentary* (Chicago: Moody Publishers, 2014), 74.

7. Rydelnik and Vanlaningham, *Moody Bible Commentary*, 74.

8. Boice, *Genesis*, 122–27.

9. Boice, *Genesis*, 122–27.

10. Boice, *Genesis*, 122–27.

11. Nancy Guthrie, *The One Year Book of Discovering Jesus in the Old Testament* (Carol Stream, IL: Tyndale House Publishers, Inc., 2010), February 15.

DAY 18

1. Theodore H. Epp, *The God of Abraham, Isaac, and Jacob* (Lincoln, NE: Back to the Bible, 1970), 100–104.

2. Nancy Guthrie, *The One Year Book of Discovering Jesus in the Old Testament* (Carol Stream, IL: Tyndale House Publishers, Inc., 2010), February 16.

3. Guthrie, *The One Year Book of Discovering Jesus in the Old Testament*, February 16.

4. Epp, *The God of Abraham, Isaac, and Jacob*, 100–104.

5. Michael Rydelnik and Michael Vanlaningham, eds., *The Moody Bible Commentary* (Chicago: Moody Publishers, 2014), 74.

6. Epp, *The God of Abraham, Isaac, and Jacob*, 100–104.

7. Epp, *The God of Abraham, Isaac, and Jacob*, 100–104.

8. Epp, *The God of Abraham, Isaac, and Jacob*, 100–104.

9. Epp, *The God of Abraham, Isaac, and Jacob*, 100–104.

DAY 19

1. James Montgomery Boice, *Genesis: An Expositional Commentary*, vol. 2 (Grand Rapids: Zondervan, 1985), 133–38.

2. Boice, *Genesis*, 133–38.

3. Angie Smith, *Seamless: Understanding the Bible as One Complete Story* (Nashville: Lifeway Press, 2020), 43.

4. Boice, *Genesis*, 139–45.

5. Boice, *Genesis*, 139–45.

6. Marty Soloman and Brent Billings, "Walking the Blood Path," December 1, 2016, in BEMA Podcast 10 audio, 49 mins 49 secs, https://www.bemadiscipleship.com/10.

7. Soloman and Billings, "Walking the Blood Path."

8. Soloman and Billings, "Walking the Blood Path."

DAY 20

1. James Montgomery Boice, *Genesis: An Expositional Commentary*, vol. 2 (Grand Rapids: Zondervan, 1985), 200–202.

DAY 21

1. Paul Wegner, "Genesis," S1112–11, Old Testament Introduction I, Los Angeles, CA, September 14 and 21, 2021.

2. Julianne Holt-Lunstad, "Testimony before the US Senate Aging Committee," April 27, 2017, https://www.aging.senate.gov/imo/media/doc/SCA_Holt_04_27_17.pdf.

3. Gary R. Collins, *Christian Counseling: A Comprehensive Guide* (Nashville: Thomas Nelson, 2007), 198.

4. "Hospitality Is about Connection, Not Perfection," *Hospitable Homemaker*, February 7, 2018, https://www.hospitablehomemaker.com/hospitality-connection-not-perfection/.

5. Henri J. M. Nowen, *Reaching Out: The Three Movements of the Spiritual Life* (New York: Crown Publishing Group, 1986), 71.

6. Rosaria Butterfield, *The Gospel Comes with a House Key: Practicing Radically Ordinary Hospitality in Our Post-Christian World* (Wheaton, IL: Crossway, 2018), 11.

DAY 22

1. Paul Wegner, "Genesis," S1112–11, Old Testament Introduction I, Los Angeles, CA, September 14 and 21, 2021.

2. James Montgomery Boice, *Genesis: An Expositional Commentary*, vol. 2 (Grand Rapids: Zondervan, 1985), 152–57.

3. Boice, *Genesis*, 152–57.

4. Boice, *Genesis*, 152–57.

5. Alicia Wong, "Women in Genesis," P2001-91, Women in Biblical Perspective, Los Angeles, CA, August 22, 2022.

6. Theodore H. Epp, *The God of Abraham, Isaac, and Jacob* (Lincoln, NE: Back to the Bible, 1970), 110–15.

7. Boice, *Genesis*, 154–57.

8. Boice, *Genesis*, 154–57.

9. Boice, *Genesis*, 154–57.

DAY 23

1. "Vaiyishtachu," accessed May 15, 2023, https://www.scribd.com/doc/71574562/יִ%D6%B4%D6%BCשׁ%D7%81תַ%D6%BC-חו%D6%BC-Vaiyishtachu-and-bowed.

2. Alicia Wong, "Women in Genesis," P2001-91, Women in Biblical Perspective, Los Angeles, CA, August 22, 2022.

3. "What Does It Mean that Job Repented in Dust and Ashes?" GotQuestions.org, accessed May 13, 2023, https://www.gotquestions.org/repent-dust-ashes.html.

4. "What Does It Mean," accessed May 13, 2023.

5. Kendell H. Easley, "2 Corinthians 6:11," *CSB Study Bible* (Wheaton, IL: Holman Bible Publishers, 2017), 1846.

6. Easley, *CSB Study Bible*, 1846.

7. *The Definition*, s.v. "vulnerability," accessed May 5, 2023, https://the-definition.com/term/vulnerability.

8. *Merriam-Webster Dictionary*, s.v. "vulnerable," accessed May 5, 2023, https://www.merriam-webster.com/dictionary/vulnerable.

9. Millie Welsh, "Made for Relationship," Cru.org, accessed May 5, 2023, https://www.cru.org/content/dam/cru/legacy/2012/02/MFR1.pdf.

10. *Merriam-Webster*, s.v. "vulnerable."

11. Michael Aalseth, "The Deep End," Cru.org, December 8, 2016, https://www.cru.org/communities/city/orangecounty/2016/the-deep-end/.

12. Welsh, "Made for Relationship."

13. Brené Brown, "Listening to Shame." TED, March 2012, https://www.ted.com/talks/brene_brown_listening_to_shame/c.

14. Brown, "Listening to Shame."

15. Charles R. Swindoll, *Koinonia Authentic Fellowship* (Frisco, TX: Insight for Living, 1985), 9.

16. Welsh, "Made for Relationship."

DAY 24

1. James Montgomery Boice, *Genesis: An Expositional Commentary*, vol. 2 (Grand Rapids: Zondervan, 1985), 158–63.

2. Boice, *Genesis*, 158–63.

3. Boice, *Genesis*, 158–63.

4. Boice, *Genesis*, 158–63.

5. Boice, *Genesis*, 158–63.

6. Theodore H. Epp, *The God of Abraham, Isaac, and Jacob* (Lincoln, NE: Back to the Bible, 1970), 115–17.

7. Epp, *The God of Abraham, Isaac, and Jacob*, 115–17.

8. Epp, *The God of Abraham, Isaac, and Jacob*, 115–17.

9. Max Lucado, *Max on Life: Discovering the Power of Prayer—4 Interactive Bible Studies* (Nashville: Thomas Nelson, 2007), overview.

10. Warren W. Wiersbe, *The Bible Exposition Commentary: New Testament,* vol. 2 (Colorado Springs: Cook Communications Ministries, 2001), 146.

11. John Piper, "Three Motivations to Pray," *Desiring God,* October 8, 2014, https://www.desiringgod.org/interviews/three-motivations-to-pray.

DAY 25

1. *Merriam-Webster,* s.v. "calling," accessed May 10, 2023, https://www.merriam-webster.com/dictionary/calling?utm_campaign=sd&utm_medium=serp&utm_source=jsonld.

2. Daniel L. Akin, *Ten Who Changed the World* (Nashville: B&H Publishing, 2012), 135.

DAY 26

1. Marty Soloman and Brent Billings, "Here I Am," December 8, 2016, in BEMA Podcast 11 audio, 53 mins 47 secs, https://www.bemadiscipleship.com/11.

2. James Montgomery Boice, *Genesis: An Expositional Commentary,* vol. 2 (Grand Rapids: Zondervan, 1985), 188–93.

3. Paul Wegner, "Genesis," S1112–11, Old Testament Introduction I, Los Angeles, CA, September 14 and 21, 2021.

4. Wegner, "Genesis."

5. Michael Rydelnik and Michael Vanlaningham, eds., *The Moody Bible Commentary* (Chicago: Moody Publishers, 2014), 70.

6. Wegner, "Genesis."

7. Boice, *Genesis,* 188–93.

8. Boice, *Genesis,* 188–93.

9. Boice, *Genesis,* 188–93.

10. Boice, *Genesis,* 188–93.

11. Boice, *Genesis,* 188–93.

12. Boice, *Genesis,* 188–93

13. Boice, *Genesis,* 188–93.

14. Boice, *Genesis*, 188–93.

15. Boice, *Genesis*, 188–93.

16. Boice, *Genesis*, 188–93.

17. Boice, *Genesis*, 188–93.

18. Boice, *Genesis*, 188–93.

19. Boice, *Genesis*, 188–93.

DAY 27

1. James Montgomery Boice, *Genesis: An Expositional Commentary*, vol. 2 (Grand Rapids: Zondervan, 1985), 194–96.

2. Boice, *Genesis*, 194–96.

3. Theodore H. Epp, *The God of Abraham, Isaac, and Jacob* (Lincoln, NE: Back to the Bible, 1970), 151.

4. Epp, *The God of Abraham, Isaac, and Jacob*, 149–51.

DAY 28

1. Nancy Guthrie, *The One Year Book of Discovering Jesus in the Old Testament* (Carol Stream, IL: Tyndale House Publishers, Inc., 2010), February 22.

2. Cru, *Satisfied?* (Peachtree City, GA: Bright Media Foundation and Campus Crusade for Christ, 2007), 8.

3. Cru, *Satisfied?*, 8.

4. Cru, *Satisfied?*, 8.

5. Cru, *Satisfied?*, 9.

6. Beth Moore, *Living Beyond Yourself: Exploring the Fruit of the Spirit—Listening Guide* (Nashville: Lifeway Press, 1998), 2.

DAY 29

1. Evan Miller, "The Four Miracles of Dunkirk," *Guideposts*, accessed May 5, 2023, https://guideposts.org/angels-and-miracles /miracles/gods-grace/the-four-miracles-of-dunkirk/.

2. Miller, "The Four Miracles of Dunkirk."

3. Walter Lord, *The Miracle of Dunkirk: The True Story of Operation Dynamo* (New York: Open Road Media, 2012).

4. Marty Soloman and Brent Billings, "Here I Am," December 8, 2016, in BEMA Podcast 11 audio, 53 mins 47 secs, https://www.bema discipleship.com/11.

5. Soloman and Billings, "Here I Am."

6. Soloman and Billings, "Here I Am."

7. James Montgomery Boice, *Genesis: An Expositional Commentary*, vol. 2 (Grand Rapids: Zondervan, 1985), 217–22.

8. Boice, *Genesis*, 217–22.

9. Boice, *Genesis*, 217–22.

10. Theodore H. Epp, *The God of Abraham, Isaac, and Jacob* (Lincoln, NE: Back to the Bible, 1970), 161–77.

11. Epp, *The God of Abraham, Isaac, and Jacob*, 161–77.

12. Epp, *The God of Abraham, Isaac, and Jacob*, 161–77.

13. Epp, *The God of Abraham, Isaac, and Jacob*, 161–77.

14. Epp, *The God of Abraham, Isaac, and Jacob*, 161–77.

15. Epp, *The God of Abraham, Isaac, and Jacob*, 161–77.

16. Epp, *The God of Abraham, Isaac, and Jacob*, 161–77.

17. Nancy Guthrie, *The One Year Book of Discovering Jesus in the Old Testament* (Carol Stream, IL: Tyndale House Publishers, Inc., 2010), February 22.

18. Guthrie, *The One Year Book of Discovering Jesus in the Old Testament*, February 23.

19. Guthrie, *The One Year Book of Discovering Jesus in the Old Testament*, February 23.

20. Guthrie, *The One Year Book of Discovering Jesus in the Old Testament*, February 23.

21. Paul Wegner, "Genesis," S1112–11, Old Testament Introduction I, Los Angeles, CA, September 14 and 21, 2021.

22. Boice, *Genesis*, 223–28.

23. Soloman and Billings, "Here I Am."

24. Boice, *Genesis*, 223–28.

DAY 30

1. Charles H. Spurgeon, *The Metropolitan Tabernacle Pulpit: Sermons Preached & Revised, During the Year 1872* (London: Passmore & Alabaster, 1873), 101.

2. C. S. Lewis, *The Chronicles of Narnia: The Last Battle* (New York: Harper Collins, 1957), 217.

3. James Montgomery Boice, *Genesis: An Expositional Commentary,* vol. 2 (Grand Rapids: Zondervan, 1985), 240–45.

4. Paul Wegner, "Genesis," S1112–11, Old Testament Introduction I, Los Angeles, CA, September 14 and 21, 2021.

5. Boice, *Genesis,* 240–45.

LOOKING FOR MORE ENCOURAGEMENT AS A MILITARY WIFE?

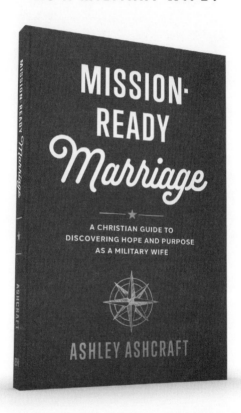

Military marriage comes with a unique set of challenges. In this book, Ashley Ashcraft guides women through these challenges and shares how she learned to find purpose and contentment as a military wife.

AVAILABLE WHERE BOOKS ARE SOLD.